BEWARE

OVERHEAD ELECTRIC POWER LINES

WARNING!

Living for fishing is one thing. Dying for it, or maiming yourself for life, is quite another. The one blot on the history and development of pole fishing in the last decade has been the number of serious accidents involving poles and overhead power lines.

The new carbon poles are frighteningly efficient at conducting electricity. They are long enough nowadays to make contact with power lines, but they do not even need to connect. Get one near enough and the power arcs across, with devastating results.

Fellow anglers have been killed. Two friends of ours have been horribly burned, and one has lost part of a leg. It should never have happened; it cannot happen to you or to us? But of course it can, unless you and we take the greatest of care.

So obey warning notices, and the advice from the electricity generating industry and the National Federation of Anglers to LOOK OUT and LOOK UP whenever you even think about setting up pole tackle in an area you are not familiar with.

Perhaps the reason why "lightning" never strikes twice is that it does not usually have to....

PLEASE DON'T DIE FOR YOUR FISHING!

My way with
THE POLE

Tom Pickering
&
Colin Dyson

PUBLICATIONS

First published in 1989 by
Pisces Angling Publications
8 Stumperlowe Close
Sheffield S10 3PP

© Colin Dyson

British Library Cataloguing in Publication Data

Pickering, Tom / Dyson, Colin
My Way With The Pole
1. Pole. Angling
I. Title
799.1'752

Hardback Edition
ISBN 0 948584 07 6

Softback Edition
ISBN 0 948584 08 4

Produced by
Angling Publications
Sheffield

Printed by
Joseph Ward and Son
Dewsbury

ACKNOWLEDGMENTS

The authors wish to thank the many people who helped us
with the production of this book.

Ken Watkins, of the National Federation of Anglers,
kindly looked through the Federation's files for missing information
about the World Championships. We also relied heavily on the files
of the former York match angler, artist and historian Frank Oates,
and the long memory of Maurice Kausman, from Huntingdon,
veteran of 45 National Championships.

We thank Dave Lumb, for coming up with all our drawings
at terribly short notice, and Rodney Coldron for his similarly
swift production of most of the photographs.

That we were able to obtain a picture of an angler from every team which
has fished European or World Championships for England is also down to
Rodney Coldron, Norman Worth and the meticulous filing of the late Colin
Graham.

We are grateful to Dave King, who founded Pisces Angling Publications
and who gave us much valuable advice and assistance
prior to publication of this book.

Last but not least we thank Tim Paisley, Steve Wilde and all at Angling
Publications
for their friendly assistance in getting us into print by the deadline.

PUBLICATIONS

My way with
THE POLE

Tom Pickering & Colin Dyson

Contents

FOREWORD

by David Bird

President, National Federation of Anglers

One of the real pleasures of being President of the National Federation of Anglers has been the privilege of attending World Championships - and seeing England win. It seems beyond belief that we ever failed to take this event seriously, but we didn't, always, as you will realise when you read this book. Nowadays we have a loyal sponsor in Steadefast, a manager who knows how to win and a terrific squad of anglers, and they and the NFA are deadly serious in ensuring that England are always there, or thereabouts, when the time comes to present the medals.

In the last two decades we have maintained our lead with traditional British float methods. We have also achieved parity with the pole, a method which has become the major growth area in match fishing. It is surprising that only three books have previously been written about the pole, and none in the last five years, when so many important developments have taken place. An update was long overdue, and who better to do it than Tom Pickering, a formidable member of our international squad and one of the most knowledgeable and highly motivated match anglers I have ever met?

And who better to help him write it than Colin Dyson, Britain's most experienced angling journalist? The two have been friends for years, and between them they have produced what I am sure will become the standard work on modern pole fishing. It also contains the only complete record of the World Championship, in terms of our results and who fished for England. For that alone it will be a valuable reference. My congratulations to them both.

The Macpherson Paints UK Angling Championship, 1988, was the latest in the long line of big match wins by the author, Tom Pickering.

INTRODUCTION

THIS MAN PICKERING

by Colin Dyson

Names come and names go in fishing, and nobody notices it more than an angling journalist, especially if one of his jobs is to monitor what is happening in match angling, nationally and locally. Names which stay around for any length of time are few indeed, and always they are the exceptional talents in a sport where almost anyone can be a king for a day. There are many good match anglers and some outstanding performers, but beyond them are the greats, and they are exceedingly rare. In my time I can count them without running out of fingers - Billy Lane, Fred Foster, Benny and Kevin Ashurst, Ivan Marks, Clive Smith... but then the memory begins to falter.

In years to come one or two more may be obvious candidates for the list, and it will surprise me if one of them is not Tom Pickering. His name has stayed in the headlines, ever since he began to make them as a junior angler. I first remember seeing it in South Yorkshire club results, and then in open events. Soon people began to talk about this young kid who was going to be something special, and when that happens in my part of the world you really do have to sit up and take notice!

Praise is hard to earn in Yorkshire pit villages, and is rarely bestowed in full measure. By the time an athlete is acknowledged to be "a bit useful" he or she is probably already in the Olympic team. The first comment I heard about Tom Pickering, the angler, was that he was "a bit useful!" He was a teenager at the time, and already the holder of a River Welland record - 51lbs of bream in four hours. At 21 he gained national attention with some amazing catches of bleak. They were impressive enough for me to want a series of articles about his techniques for Coarse Angler magazine, and I contacted him for the first time.

All I knew about him then was his record, and that he was a trainee miner at South Kirkby Colliery. The mind has the unfortunate habit of categorising people we do not know. It uses available information to form a mental picture which often turns out to be remarkably accurate. I expected a diffident person, possibly a bit unsure of himself. I guessed it might be difficult to extract the relevant information, or enough to make the magazine features interesting. Surely, though, there would have to be at least one good article in a kid who could blitz 35lbs of bleak in five hours...?

It took only a few seconds to realise, when I finally did meet him, that my image-making mechanism had malfunctioned. If this was a miner, I thought, he must spend all day banging his head on the roof supports! He was way over 6ft tall, and built like a beanpole. He was about as diffident as Jimmy Saville, and as unsure as Terry Wogan! As for the difficulty of extracting useful information, it poured out so fast that the shorthand note, which had served me reasonably well during a lifetime in journalism, was suddenly quite inadequate. Even as a youngster Tom had some sort of fast-forward button in the brain, and I began to pity his opposition.

If I make him sound to be cocky and brash, forget it. He wasn't like that then, nor is he now. He was just a very confident youngster who knew exactly where he was going, and I knew right then that he would not be down the pit for much longer. Tom clearly had a gift for remembering everything he had ever learned about fishing, and the ability to apply it. From an early age he had been under the wing of Denis White, a match angler who ranked with the best, though at the time relatively few outside the Barnsley area had ever heard of him. Ironically it was to be the success of the pupil which eventually drew attention to the teacher, though that was no accident.

Tom made it happen. He would never take the credit for anything, if it had emanated from Denis, and in the early days much of it did. Eventually they became a couple of clones. One had absorbed all the other could impart, and they went on learning together, expanding their frontiers of knowledge to the point where, as a pair, they ranked below no other angling double act, in my opinion. Small wonder, then, that Tommy felt uncomfortable when it was he who was first catapulted to fame by the aforementioned articles about bleak fishing.

I think it was the content of the features, coupled with his obvious ability, which did it, but Tom does not agree. He puts it down to the catchphrase I invented for him in that series. I called him "the Bionic Bleaker," and it stuck. Maybe he is right about it, for the nickname seemed to draw attention to him at a time when he could not stop winning open events and, later, some of the major invitation matches. The Barnsley team were, at the time, beginning to emerge as a major force in the National Championship, and that did him no harm either. One way or another Tom Pickering was forever in the headlines, and was an obvious candidate to fish for England.

He got the treasured call from Stan Smith, then manager of the England World Championship team, for the match in Austria in 1978. Denis White was called the following year, and both of them fished in the first England team to win gold medals in Italy in 1985. To add extra spice to the occasion they both won their sections, despite being pegged next to Italians, backed by fiercely partisan crowds. In less than a decade Tommy had gone from the bottom of a pit to the top of the world!

In that decade and since, of course, the pole method has played an increasingly important role in improving Tom's record. He is not obsessive about it, but if this approach is considered to be the best for a particular venue, on a certain day, he will use it. He has made the pole work well for him everywhere the method is a viable proposition, and those fortunate enough to hear him speak about his methods at his popular roadshows are invariably surprised by the depth of his knowledge - not to mention the machinegun style of delivery! But it's a bit like listening to a stand-up comic all night. He has you rolling in the aisles, but next day you remember only a couple of the jokes!

Often Tom has been asked, after his shows, if he has a book where it is all written down, and that is part of the reason why we are now cooperating to produce one. An update on the art of pole fishing is long overdue, and we will attempt to cover every aspect of it. We will also look at the history of pole fishing as it relates to the World Championships, detailing all the results and England placings up to the present time. We name every angler who has represented his country at world level, something which has never been put into print before. Many of them marched into hopeless battle, for reasons explained in the relevant chapter, but between them they helped us to realise that the pole method had to be totally mastered, if England were to become a major force at international level.

That realisation eventually became a crusade. England have now been champions three times under the present manager Dick Clegg, but that is no longer enough. Clegg and his battle-hardened squad of internationals have another and more important ambition - to win a world title on the pole; to beat the continentals at their own game. In the not so distant past that would have seemed like a mere pipe dream. Kevin Ashurst never even hinted at that possibility in the excellent book "The Encyclopaedia of Pole Fishing," which he wrote in conjunction with my late colleague Colin Graham. That book was published only in 1983, but in terms of the development of pole fishing in Britain that was light years ago.

So much has happened since. Kevin himself, and the other leading internationals, have mastered vastly better and ever longer poles, but behind them are great numbers of new pole anglers, working the open circuit and extending right down into the pub and club match scene. The method is here to stay, and once we have a generation of anglers who have grown up with the pole we are on the same footing as the top continentals. Whether we can win a world title on the pole in the interim remains to be seen, but I, for one, would not bet against it.

There is a great hunger for information about the pole techniques, and the aim of this book is to provide all that is currently available. As I write this the job is still before us, and it seems a daunting but fascinating proposition.

THE ORIGINS OF POLE FISHING

by Colin Dyson

In one sense pole fishing is as old as angling itself, for rods and lines were in use here long before the invention of the reel. It is arguable, therefore, when pole fishing in a manner similar to today's was first employed, but it was probably around the middle of the last century. The veteran Cambridge angler Maurice Kausman tells me he once owned a pole with this inscription on the butt ferrule: "Presented to a West End angler for saving another from drowning in the Grand Union Canal - 1860."

Roach poles were, says Maurice, a favourite with Lee and Thames anglers from about that time until shortly after the first World War, when the "Sheffield style," with short rods and running tackle, took the angling world by storm. The poles, certainly those most sought after, were made by Fred Sowerbutts the East London tackle dealer, and before him by his wife's father. Fred's real name was Warren, but he changed to his wife's maiden name to preserve the business name. Sowerbutts, therefore, were around for a considerable time.

The poles were made from tonkin cane with bamboo butts, and with built cane or whalebone tips. Usually they were in four sections, with overall lengths anything from 18 feet to 21 feet 6 inches. They had ferrules invariably made from German silver, and they were fitted with rings at the tip and another, whipped about half way down the top joint, to which the line was tied.

Maurice remembers that one of the methods which succeeded when the Lee had little movement was to bait with breadcrust, squeezed around with finely ground breadcrumbs. These disintegrated in the water, leaving the crust "kernel" inside to lure the fish attracted to the white "cloud." The bait was lowered into the water, rather than cast, and it was deadly for the roach. Lee anglers were noted for their dexterity and skill with this method. As is the case today, however, some were better than others. Maurice wonders if there is anyone alive today who remembers Johnny Osborne or Teddy Vincent, who were highly regarded as Lee experts with the pole. On the Thames one Charlie Baxter was the big name with the same method. He was noted for big catches of roach to 2lbs plus from Hartslock Woods, near Pangbourne, especially at flood time.

The present day use of elastic is, says Maurice, an extension of the whalebone

7

tip system which enabled anglers at Taplow to play and land barbel, when hempseed fishing became the rage just after the first war. They played out the fish with the full length of the poles, unshipping the butt sections just before the fish were netted. Clearly the weight of those poles prevented their use for all the methods pole anglers employ nowadays. They were not so much used for swimming the stream. More commonly they were held in iron hooks, driven into the ground. Lines were fixed to fish over depth with floats, of course, to signal the bites - a kind of laying-on, or float-legering.

Had it not been for the success of the Sheffield style of fishing with rods and reels pole fishing might have continued to develop here, much as it did in some of the continental countries. Instead the method faded out of use almost completely here until we saw a mini-revival in the south in the 1960s and Kevin Ashurst's "conversion" in 1970. Since then we have seen interest in the method accelerating at a remarkable speed, especially with the advent of good carbon poles in the present decade.

Whether British anglers missed anything by losing the pole method for 40 years or so is open to debate, but on balance I think they gained from it. We went on to build on that Sheffield style, improving our float-fishing techniques over the years and deriving tremendous benefit from the development of better reels and lighter and longer rods as new materials became available. We also saw some remarkable advances in legering techniques, notably the invention or, as some would have it, the re-invention of the swingtip and quivertip. We saw, too, the revival of the swimfeeder and, eventually, the total sophistication of that method. We learned so much about fishing and the behaviour of fish that when the pole method returned our top anglers were able to adapt to it with remarkable speed.

It presented them with an easier and more efficient way of fishing at close range, though to some of us wielding 8 metres of heavy glass pole was a daunting prospect! The continentals had the edge when it came to combining sheer strength with delicacy of bait presentation, but lost most of it with the advent of carbon. Suddenly we were all learning to use the longer and lighter poles at the same time, and the century or so of knowledge anglers like the French and Belgians had to call upon was virtually nullified in a decade. But we still had an awesome lead with rod and reel, and the benefits of that are to be seen in the World Championship results over the last few years.

It is only a matter of time before we win that match on the pole, and we may see a continental victory on rod and reel sooner than many may imagine - probably by the Italians, who have worked very hard with waggler float techniques. The next few years will be very interesting.

CHOOSING
THE RIGHT POLE

by Tom Pickering

It is pointless to begin the instructional section of this book with long explanations of the merits of pole fishing. Most readers will have bought or borrowed the book because they are already into pole fishing and want to learn more. Others will have already realised at least some of the advantages, and will want to start on the right foot, but there will be some who are coming to the game with no knowledge or experience. For their benefit, in particular, a short summary is necessary. The pole system, properly employed, will catch small fish at close range far faster than rod and reel fishing, and this book will explain exactly how it is done. Within the limits of its own length a pole will present lighter floats and terminal tackles with greater delicacy than is possible with rod and reel at the same range, except, perhaps, in the most perfect of conditions. Within the same limits the pole will give you more effective fishing time, simply because there is less need for casting and retrieving, and the bait is presented in the right place much longer. The pole attracts bites more easily and strikes them more effectively. And, providing they are properly set up, poles will prove more efficient, in the playing and landing of good fish, than any other angling method.

In match fishing terms the pole offers greater speed, especially when it is employed "fishing to hand" - the expression we have come to use for fishing an overall length of line roughly equivalent to the length of pole employed (see picture overleaf). This means fish can be hooked and swung directly to hand, providing, of course, that they are not too big to be landed in that way. But, for the reasons outlined above, there is also speed in the other main method - the short line system. That is the description of the method of using a length of line shorter, sometimes much shorter, than the pole. A typical situation is that we can use, say, 10ft of line to fish an 8ft deep swim at a range of 10+ metres. To land fish hooked in this way the pole has to be fed smoothly backwards and taken apart at the appropriate length for landing that fish. That operation is known as "unshipping," and is fully dealt with in both words and pictures later on.

(A brief explanatory note. Throughout this book there will be a conflict between metric measurement and feet and inches. I think metric with poles because they are sold in metre lengths, but I grew up with feet and inches. So

A somewhat bad example of fishing to hand. The line should really be longer, so that the full length of the pole can be employed.

did most current pole anglers, other than those who have left school in the past year or so. We are in a transitionary period in which some will be confused, whatever I do. Apologies to the metric-minded, who will have to mentally convert my depths and tackle rig measurements. Think of six inches as 15cm, a foot as 30cm and a metre as a bit more than 3ft).

The pole method has an "image problem" for those who have not tried it, simply because it looks unwieldy and, possibly, hard work. There is little doubt that it qualified on both counts in the early days, when we were struggling with up to 8 metres of heavy fibre glass, though even then there were many who were sufficiently impressed with the advantages to suffer the drawbacks. The bandwagon got rolling merrily along, even with the inferior equipment, but there is little doubt that the current boom in pole fishing gathered its real momentum from the development of much better, lighter, longer, stronger and more rigid poles made from carbon fibre. Today's best poles, at lengths of 14 metres, feel, in use, very much like those early 8 metre glass jobs, and they are vastly more efficient. Drop back to 11 or 12 metres and most anglers can cope perfectly well. At 8 to 10 metres, which are probably the lengths most often employed, it's a piece of cake for virtually anyone. It is that which has really set the game alight, and the method really ought to carry a health warning. It is addictive in the extreme. I do not know one angler who has bought a carbon pole who has not fallen madly in love with the method!

I know few, either, who have bought a glass pole for economy reasons and who have not come back into my shop to buy a more expensive carbon job a short time afterwards. Most glass poles end up as spares for short range, small fish work at 3 to 4 metres, with the thicker two sections converted into telescopic landing net handles. For that reason I try to talk anglers out of buying them. If they come in with £40 to £50 for an 8 metre glass pole I try to tell them that £70 to £80 will get them a vastly superior 8 metre carbon. It may sound as though I am after more profit, but in fact I get less, for I know the great majority of glass buyers end up buying twice. Mind you, quite a few of those who buy 8 metres of carbon also come back, eventually, to pay hundreds of pounds for the longer carbons. For some of them it's a real struggle, and I often wish somebody could come up with a good, long pole more in line with the pockets of the majority. Sadly, I don't think that can happen, at least for a long time. Prices range into four figures for the wealthy and the utterly dedicated, but they are not gaining all that much over those who shop in the £250 to £400 bracket, the current price range for some excellent 11 metre poles.

I realise I am talking telephone numbers as far as some anglers are concerned, but that's the reality of the upper end of the range. Thankfully it is possible to get into pole fishing much cheaper than that. I would advise newcomers to buy glass if they are genuinely unsure whether they will like the method, but to really think hard about finding an extra £30 or so for an 8 metre carbon. Even if they find they don't enjoy it they will have no trouble selling it on to another aspiring pole man, and they won't lose very much. For those who are already sold on the method the advice is the same as it has been for years in the rod and reel area - buy the best you can afford.

It would be wrong for me to deal with actual makes of poles, but I have some very firm ideas about the best types. It is not a good idea to buy a telescopic pole, except, possibly, a short one for bleak and other small fish. They are perfectly OK for that job, but at longer lengths they become sloppy after a bit of use, and rigidity is one of the merits we mostly require in a pole. They are no good for landing bonus big fish, for reasons which will emerge later, and I can't think of many situations in which a telescopic pole would be as good or as versatile as a take apart pole of the same length. I have, however, noticed the Italian bleak men using telescopics in longer lengths, possibly because they get easier in the action as they wear. The softer pole and flicktip top may help them with the casting of the very light floats they tend to use.

Unfortunately I now have to become more technical, in recommending the best type of pole. The two basic types are known as "put-ins" and "put-overs," and the descriptions are not very clear. They refer to the way the poles fit together, and in one sense they are all "put-ins," for we always have to put one section into another. The question is, which way round is best? The "put-in" has the second section fitting into the butt section, and so on to the end, or near the end, and the "put-over" has it the other way around (see Fig 1). The latter system, in my opinion, is usually better than the other, and for several different reasons.

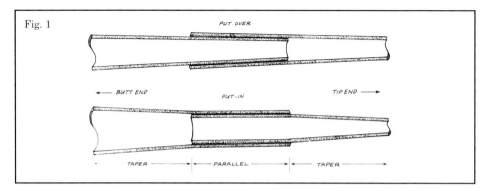

Fig. 1

PUT OVER

← BUTT END   PUT-IN   TIP END →

TAPER ——→|←— PARALLEL —→|←— TAPER —→

Of the two assembly systems, the put-over (top) is vastly superior.

First of all the "put-in" type has to be a perfect fit, in the same way as a match rod ferrule. It it wasn't a good fit the pole would "knock" in use, just like a worn ferrule. The joint which is tight enough not to knock, however, is quite likely to jam up, particularly when wet. Water acts as a lubricant, and the joint can slide together just that bit further than intended. At best it can be difficult to take the pole apart in order to land a fish when using the short line system. At worst it can be so tight you cannot get it apart. Anglers marching to the next swim for assistance are a common sight, and sometimes we see them coming back to match HQ with two sections still welded together! All it can take to stick fast, sometimes, is a bit of grit, even if it hasn't been pushed together too far.

Consider, now, the problem of shipping the pole - putting it together. Assembly of the "put-in" type requires you to line up the male and female joints exactly, before pushing them home. Now that's no problem when you are assembling the pole prior to fishing, but there are times when we have to add a section while fishing. When you have landed a fish by unshipping it has to go back together again, and at times we also have to add sections to play a good fish more easily. We might want to push it further out, away from nearside snags

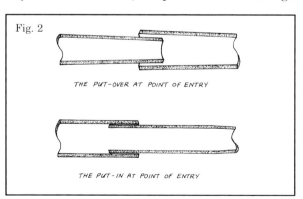

Fig. 2

THE PUT-OVER AT POINT OF ENTRY

THE PUT-IN AT POINT OF ENTRY

Differences in diameters at the entry point make the put-over much easier to assemble.

or weedbeds until some of the fight has been taken out of it. Think of the difficulty then in having to line up the joints exactly. It is an awkward job, and if it doesn't go right in the female joint can splinter under the strain. With the "put-over" joint these problems diminish. The end of the male joint is smaller in diameter than the hole it has to enter (see Fig 2), and you can find it from an angle without having to line it up exactly. It isn't a good fit until it is properly pushed home, and while they can jam, in theory, just the same as the other type, they do not seem to do so. The other plus for the "put-over" is the wear factor. When the "put-in" joint wears it becomes loose, and knocks. When the "put-over" wears it simply goes in further, and remains a good fit.

I would hesitate before buying anything but a "put-over," and would have been even more emphatic than that had I not recently examined the prototype of a new "put-in" pole which handled beautifully. It was so good I might consider putting up with the difficulties of shipping and unshipping if it comes onto the market, but right now I'm a put-over man. What length should you buy? If you can afford an 11 metre buy it. They are quite light at that length now, though $12^1/_2$ and 14 metre jobs are a handful for some. All the longer poles have one common characteristic - they are a delight to use one section short of the maximum length, and when you have two sections off you hardly know you are holding one, once you have sorted out the right way to handle a pole.

You will find that poles differ at the thin end. The top two and sometimes three sections are usually telescopic, and there is a good reason for that. They cannot pull off, and that used to happen a lot before they were made telescopic. It could occur when playing a fish, if the angler made a mistake and played it with the pole held too low, or when trying a direct pull to free snagged tackle. That's never a good idea. If you are snagged really fast feed the pole back until you can get hold of the line (not always possible when using long poles), or the elastic, the use of which I will come to shortly. If you cannot reach the line or elastic then unship to the telescopic section. That way you won't lose any of your pole if you have to pull for a break.

Poles usually come, too, with two and sometimes three end sections. There may be two sections to fit together telescopically, plus a flicktip. This is made from solid carbon fibre, very much like the tips used on quivertip rods, and this feeds through the other two sections to make a three piece telescopic end section. On the cheaper poles that's it, and you have to decide whether you want that three piece flicktip at the end or whether to have the two hollow end sections rigged up for an elastic system (next chapter). Swapping around between the two is a pain, and most anglers will buy two more end pieces in order to have both options easily available.

Some of the more expensive poles come with alternative end sections, and since most anglers who can afford these already have a short flicktip pole, they will rig up these sections with two different strengths of elastic.

Shipping a put-over pole.

FLICKTIPS & ELASTIC SYSTEMS

by Tom Pickering

Very little in pole fishing has changed much more in recent years than the way we rig up with our flicktips and elastic systems. At first the safest way of tackling up for the flicktip was to whip a tiny ring on the end and loop the terminal tackle to that. There wasn't a lot wrong with that for the glass poles, except the occasional problem of the line tangling around the ring, but with the later carbon poles the rings had to be really tiny to pass through the hollow sections at the end of the pole. We therefore had to look for a quicker and more simple way of doing the job and avoiding the problems.

The ultimate answer was to jam the line on to the end of the flicktip with two tight silicone rubber or plastic sleeves, preferably the latter. We can buy them in different sizes for the attachment of pole floats, and rigging up with them could not be much more easy. I put a $1\frac{1}{2}$" long sleeve and a short one on the line above the float, before I put the tackle on a winder (a subject to be dealt with shortly). I pass the short sleeve over the end of the flicktip, which is obviously very thin in diameter, and with the line through the sleeve I force the sleeve along the tip until it is very tight indeed. Then I take the line a few turns around the tip and jam on the longer sleeve, leaving some of it overlapping the end of the flicktip. (Fig 3).

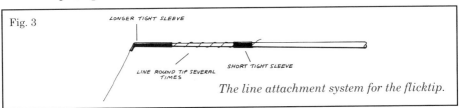

Fig. 3

LONGER TIGHT SLEEVE

SHORT TIGHT SLEEVE

LINE ROUND TIP SEVERAL TIMES

The line attachment system for the flicktip.

Having that sleeve protruding for a short distance seems to cure the tangle problem completely, and while it may not sound all that secure as a method of attachment I can assure you that it is. You might be able to pull it out, exerting a direct and steady pull, but there is no way a fish can do it. With rare exceptions we are fishing only for the small fish with the flicktip, but even if you hook a much bigger one by accident it won't shift the line out of the sleeves with an angled pull. The line would break before that could happen.

When bigger fish are likely to show, or when we are actually fishing for them deliberately, we obviously need a way of avoiding line breaks. With no reel, or any means of giving line to a running fish, we have to use elastic as a shock absorber and, in effect, as a virtually automated means of playing them to a standstill. I will deal with that in more detail shortly, after describing the best ways of rigging up the pole with an efficient elastic system.

The first method most pole anglers used was to attach it to an aluminium or fibre glass crook, which had to be made to fit very tightly into or onto the end of the last hollow section of the pole. The drawbacks with that system were numerous. For one thing the crook could come off, and the fibre glass ones broke too easily. If you are thinking of employing the crook take care to use the alloy type, but I really don't recommend the crook system. A significant handicap is that the elastic has to hang below the pole, which does not help your float control, especially in a wind. In fact, if you use sufficient elastic to do an efficient job on a good fish there is far too much of it hanging down. Quite apart from making proper float control an almost hopeless proposition the dangling elastic and the crook combine to produce tangle problems.

No, crooks really belong in Wormwood Scrubs; their namesakes have no major role in modern pole fishing. There is one plus point for crooks, though, which no other system has yet managed to match. The method is totally friction free, and makes better use of a given length of elastic than any other method. Sadly the drawbacks far outweigh that one advantage.

I believe it was southern pole anglers who came up with at least part of the answer, inventing a way of putting 3 to 4ft of elastic - the length required for maximum efficiency - inside the top two sections of the pole. It ran from a base plug set-up at the thick end through a brass or plastic bush at the tip. At the time it was considered brilliant, for it kept the elastic out of the influence of the wind, and enabled us to use enough of it to do a proper job. The one big drawback was friction, which could easily be felt when a good fish pulled the elastic out through the bush. Naturally it was northern anglers who perfected the system by using bushes made from PTFE, a slippery material said to have self-lubricating qualities. Whether that's true I'm not sure, but I do know that it made a vast difference to the friction problem, even though it has not completely eliminated it. To begin with the PTFE bushes fitted externally, but when tackle manufacturers picked up the idea one of them eventually came up with a

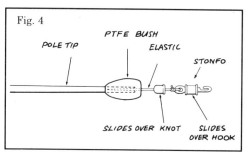

Fig. 4

POLE TIP   PTFE BUSH   ELASTIC   STONFO

SLIDES OVER KNOT   SLIDES OVER HOOK

The original home-made external PTFE bush system. Nowadays anglers can buy ready-made bushes with a neater cylindrical shape, but all the rest is standard.

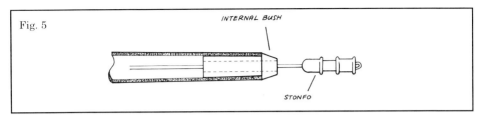

The alternative internal PTFE bush system is neater and more efficient.

smaller and neater bush which fitted internally, which I reckon is vastly better. The drawings (Figs 4 and 5, and the pictures below), show both types. There is nothing to tangle around, with the internal system, and elastic is delivered very smoothly, especially if it is treated before use with the special lubricant which is also available now.

For more experienced pole anglers I ought to say why I think the internal bush is better, because I know some of them prefer the external types. The internal bush plugs into the end of the pole, and you have to cut the pole back a few inches until the diameter is right to take the insert. Losing a few inches of often expensive pole seems a waste, but you do gain something by doing it. It widens the hole at the end of the pole, and assists the smooth delivery of elastic through the bush. The external bushes fit onto much thinner pole section. It can be just about the same diameter as the stronger elastic, and there is bound to be resistance. Even thinner elastic can be hampered by water or a bit of grit in the end of the pole. I used to wonder why the internal bush seemed more friction free, but it was England international Alan McAtee who provided the answer - that difference in diameter at the end of the pole. It's only a few thousandths of an inch, but it makes a big difference.

Around the same time as the internal bush appeared we also got the best method to date for the back end of the system. It's a plastic cone-shaped plug, the Uni-Bung, which has a strong piece of nylon monofilament through the middle, and a hole at the front end to take the elastic. It is made to fit any size and internal diameter of pole. You simply have to cut it down from the thick end (taking great care not to cut through the nylon monofilament) until the cone fits just far enough inside the pole. You have to remember that the next section has

The external and internal bush systems, one showing line attachment to the Stonfo.

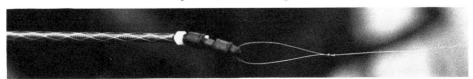

to fit into it, so leave enough room. When the job is done the monofilament acts as a tab, enabling easy removal of the cone for renewal or adjustment of the elastic. Cut the tab down so a couple of inches protrudes beyond the end of the pole section. There is a drawing here (Fig 6) of what I consider to be the best internal set-up, for anyone who wants to use it.

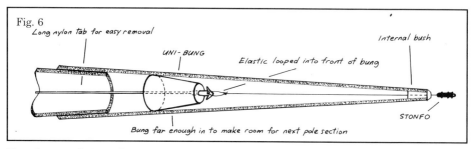

Fig. 6
Long nylon tab for easy removal

UNI-BUNG

Elastic looped into front of bung

Internal bush

STONFO

Bung far enough in to make room for next pole section

Foreshortened view of a complete internal elastic system.

The method of feeding elastic through the end sections for this system is simple when the pole is dry. You can simply drop it through when rigging up at home, but you will find if you ever have to repair a break on the bank that it will not feed through when the inside of the pole is wet. You will need a special threader, which makes the job dead easy (described in the Accessories chapter). The most important thing at this stage is the knot required to attach the elastic to the Super Stonfo, which is the clever little gadget connecting the terminal tackle to the elastic system. The Stonfo (illustrated in Figs 4 and 7) has a hook at the front end, which the pole tackle is looped over, and a sliding fitting which pushes over the hook to make everything secure in use. At the rear end of the Stonfo is a removable cap which is threaded up the elastic before you tie the knot. With this cap off you will see a hole in the Stonfo and a curved recess where the finished knot is intended to lie.

Hopefully the knot drawing (Fig 7) will help to make sense of the written instructions, which might seem a bit complicated, but this is what you do. Put about 3" of the elastic through the hole and lay the end alongside the main length of elastic. You now have the Stonfo hanging off a simple loop. Now make

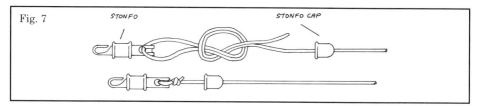

Fig. 7
STONFO
STONFO CAP

The simple elastic knot for the Stonfo before and after being snugged up tight.

a loop with the doubled elastic and pass the Stonfo through that loop. Slowly tighten the resulting knot, carefully snugging it up until it butts up into the recess on the Stonfo. Do it very carefully, giving it a final tighten before trimming off the loose end, leaving a stub of about one eighth of an inch long.

Ex-Boy Scouts will realise that all it involves is the first half of a simple granny or reef knot, tied with a double length of "rope," but assisted by the elasticity of the material itself the knot is very secure. The aim is to make the knot small and neat enough for the end cap to be brought down over the knot and pushed back into place. If it won't push back properly the knot is a bit too bulky, and will need to be re-tied.

Always tie the Stonfo on first, then take the elastic through the pole for attachment to the hole in the tapered Uni-Bung device. The job is easier than it is at the front end, except that the elastic has to be properly tensioned - not too tight or too slack. Cut the elastic an inch or two beyond the length of the pole sections you are working with, and put it through the hole in the front end of the bung. Pull a few inches through so you have it under tension, and tie the same knot you did at the front end. The job is much easier, incidentally, if you "collapse" the telescopic section (i.e. shorten it) before you actually tie this knot. Then, if you let go accidentally, the elastic will not vanish down the hole! There is no need to snug the knot right up to the bung, as you did with the Stonfo. Just make a loop with the doubled end, take the plug through it and pull tight. Extend the pole again, and push the bung into the pole section to its right position, and test the result. The Stonfo should be pulled up against the tip of the pole, with no elastic hanging out. If it is too slack, re-tie at the bung end, but if the tension seems too great you will have to start again with a new piece of elastic. It should be obvious to err on the slack side to start with, but after a while you will get it right at the first or second attempt. Sometimes, after you have caught a few fish, the elastic will stretch a bit, and hang out of the end of the pole. Try dipping it in the water, and if it doesn't go back by itself spend a few moments shortening the elastic, as described. Match anglers, for whom time is precious, should really take a few spare lengths of elastic with Stonfos already attached. Then, with the help of a threader, it is a quick and simple job to replace a broken elastic.

I know, I haven't yet dealt with the types and strengths of elastics, but I will do that after mentioning the other elastic system which is now in common use - the external method which is used in association with the flicktip. Some anglers prefer this to the internal approach, and there is an argument in its favour. It probably delivers elastic more smoothly, and it is more adjustable in use, for reasons I will deal with after describing it. The drawing (Fig 8) makes most of the points. We have spare tip sections of the pole plus the flicktip, with

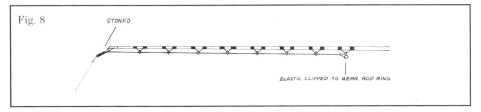

Fig. 8

STONFO

ELASTIC CLIPPED TO REAR ROD RING

The external elastic system.

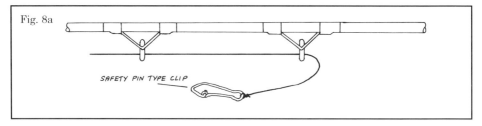

External elastic can be quickly tightened or slackened by clipping to another ring.

tiny rings taped or whipped on every 3 to 4 inches. We have the Stonfo at the front end, again, and a similar length of elastic, fastened to one of the rings towards the end.

I suppose we are mainly talking about an insurance system for the flicktip, where it is used for its normal purpose of catching small fish but where the occasional bigger fish might turn up. One good example is the Leeds/Liverpool Canal, where in matches you need to be fishing for gudgeon or other small fish. But there is a good chance, on this water, of hooking a carp, a tench or even a good perch. On the flicktip alone the chances are you will not land these fish. The flicktip and the pole will bend as far as they can go, and the line will break or a small hook will simply pull out. The back-up of elastic makes it a different ball game. You do have a good chance of landing the bonus fish, and they are frequently the difference between winning and losing.

Obviously you don't want to give elastic to little fish like gudgeon, so the advice is to fish this system with the elastic a bit tighter than it is when used in an internal system. You should use elastic strong enough for the better fish in the water. There is little point using weak stuff when you only want the elastic as emergency back-up. If it is not strong enough to cope with an emergency you will look a bit silly!

On the internal system we mostly choose a strength of elastic to cope with the size of fish we are expecting to catch, though some anglers have the same approach with the external method as well. The rod ring system is certainly versatile in some respects, for you can move the elastic from one ring to another in a matter of seconds to increase or decrease the tension. One way is to take the elastic, looped at the end, through all the rings except the last one. Then you can fix it by taking the loop over the pole section, positioning it at the back of the last but one ring. To increase tension you re-fix it over the last ring; to reduce tension unthread it from the original ring and re-fix at the third ring from the end. Another way is to take the elastic, looped again, through the rings and then back to loop over the last but one ring. Adjustment, then, is a simple matter of moving back a ring or forward a ring, much the same as before. Yet another method, and probably the most simple of them all, is to tie the back end of the elastic to a safety-pin type clip, which can be attached to any ring to tighten or slacken the elastic (Fig 8a). The only drawback of the external method is that the ringed section has to be carried separately from the rest of the pole, but that's not much of a problem.

CHOICE OF ELASTICS

by Tom Pickering

One thing newcomers to pole fishing find quite amazing is the efficiency of one of the aspects of the game which they are initially a bit worried about - playing good quality fish on the elastic. For anglers brought up to learn the delicate skills of playing fish off the reel, either by using the slipping clutch or by backwinding at precisely the right moment, it is difficult to imagine just sitting there and allowing elastic to do the work. That is virtually what happens. We might "follow" a fish with the pole, moving it right to left or left to right, fondly imagining that we are assisting the elastic to perform its shock absorbing role, but the result would probably be the same, in all but a few cases, if we simply held the pole stock still! Adding a section or two to give ourselves more playing room with a good fish is a valid tactic (more about that later), but most of the time the elastic is on its own.

A remarkably good job it does, too. When I was discussing with Colin Dyson how to explain its efficiency we came up with a few analogies. Possibly the best is an imaginary situation, in which an angler is tied at the waist with a length of very powerful elastic, anchored to a tree. If he tried to get away, either by running or walking, he would only get so far before he was slowed down, stopped and then drawn backwards towards the anchor point. At no time would he be able to generate enough speed and power to break the elastic because of the smooth and progressive way the power of the elastic is applied. Tied with some other material of the same breaking strain, but with little or no elasticity, he might be able to run very fast and smash free. That's what happens, in effect, when we hook an unexpectedly big fish on the flicktip, and it is the progressive power of well-chosen elastic which helps us to defeat big fish hooked on the pole.

Where can we look for supreme examples of the capabilities of elastic? Most anglers would concede that carp are the hardest fighting of our coarse fish, but carp well into double figures have been landed on poles. The biggest I know of was over 17lbs, but there may have been one or two even bigger than that. Once a carp has been stopped by elastic, its chances of escape are diminished. Some of its energy will have been expended, and the first run is its best chance. Thereafter its runs will become shorter and shorter, and if it doesn't snag up, and the hook-hold doesn't wear out, it's as good as in the net. Scale down from

*Elastic being tested
to the limit by a
Mallory Park carp.*

there and you have the same story with any other fish.

Clearly, then, the correct choice of elastic is important, but it is an area where a lot of anglers are confused. I hope I can put them right here, by describing my approach to the problem. First of all it is important to have elastic of the right quality, and there are two types I know of which meet that requirement. One is ZIM, which comes in eight sizes numbered 1 to 8. The other comes on colour coded winders, red being the weakest. It goes progressively stronger through green, blue, black and white. My personal preference is the ZIM, though there is one slight reservation. I have discovered, lately, that there can be spooling errors with it. On the odd occasion I have found the same diameter of elastic as two different numbers, which is obviously a mistake by either the makers or those who package it for sale. I'm hoping it is a limited mistake, for it is not

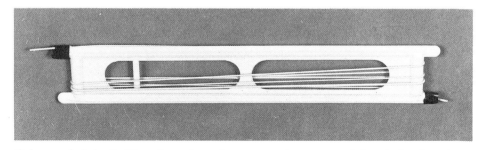

Colour-coded elastic (the coloured markers are on the corners of the winder frame).

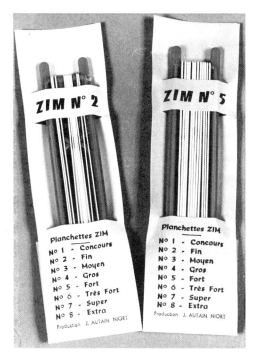

Two sizes of ZIM elastic.

something an inexperienced angler will be able to spot, and maybe some tackle dealers don't notice it either. I discovered it because I am a pole angler myself, but how can I advise readers how to avoid the possible trap? All I can suggest is that you ask for a particular number, and then ask to see the one below and the one above. If they aren't all a different thickness then one of them is wrongly labelled.

Now that little proviso is out of the way I shall summarise the basic approach to correct choice of elastics, and at the end of this section of the book I will produce some of the key bits of information in the form of a table, for easy reference later. There are other factors to take into account, quite apart from the elastic itself. The whole set-up has to be balanced to the right breaking strains of hook length and main line and, of course, to hook size as well. For the moment, though, I will quickly go through the different sizes of elastic, and which situations they are used in.

Starting with the ZIM, I never use number 1, which is very fine indeed, though some anglers may have special use for it for very tiny fish. There are times when these mini fish are bumped off on flicktip tackle, and I suppose ultra fine elastic coming even a short distance out of the pole might just make the difference. Up to now, however, I have not found a venue where I think it might be useful to me.

The number 2 is what I use the most, for a variety of venues - mostly bloodworm fishing on canals like the Oxford and the Bridgewater, places where you are not going to be catching fish much over 3 to 4oz. A half ounce gudgeon might pull it out six inches. A 4oz fish might bring it out 2ft. That's a key point you should take note of. If your choice of elastic is right then the fish you are catching must make the elastic function. If you have it wrong, using say number 5 elastic for this job, the elastic won't come out, the fish will make the pole tip bounce and it could come off the hook. So let the fish pull and stretch the elastic; that's what it's all about.

The number 3 elastic is another I use a fair bit. This is for waters where the fish are a bit bigger, like the Stainforth & Keadby Canal. You can catch roach to 10oz, small chub and eels. Even the small fish are around 1oz, so the elastic is upgraded a little bit. Those small fish will pull about 6" of elastic, the bigger ones 2ft, which leaves plenty in hand for the odd bonus fish which is even bigger, like a bream or one of the better chub. I might land them after a bit of a struggle, but why struggle with the sizes of fish I expect to catch? If I used the number 2 elastic here the average fish would take too much elastic. You can't control them properly, and they just swim around stretching the elastic and taking up valuable match fishing time!

When it comes to number 4 and 5 elastics, I have never found a great deal of difference, but there is a bit, so we might as well take advantage of it. The number 4 I use on most sections of the non-tidal Trent, though especially at Long Higgin. There are a lot of small fish at Higgin, but you can also expect a chub or two, and some better roach. Most of the fish are similar in size to those on the Stainforth & Keadby, but here they have some flow to help them, so we go up a number. The number 5 I also use on the Trent where there are bigger fish and/or heavier flow, like Holme Marsh, for example, or on the tidal river at places like Collingham. You might think I am being a bit too choosy, here, but it is important to get it right. You step up when there is a good reason to.

Sizes 6 and 7 I will use where tench can be expected, or small carp. Both species are going to pull a good bit of elastic out, even numbers 6 and 7, so you might as well make it harder for them. Number 8 is very strong stuff, and I have never had to use it up to now. The only reason I would use number 8 would be if I was in a very snaggy swim and the only way I could fish it was with a pole. It hasn't happened yet, but one day I might draw such a swim on a river, with barbel or big chub which have to be struck and lifted very quickly to get them clear of a snag.

To deal with the colour coded elastic now, it may be the same stuff as ZIM, marketed in a different way. Certainly I can see no difference between the red code and number 2, the green and number 4, the blue and 5, the black and 7 and the white and 8. You therefore use them for the same jobs I have just described for the numbered elastics.

ELASTICS AT A GLANCE

ZIM number	Colour coded	Hook length	Main line	Hook sizes
1	–	8oz	1lb	26 or 24
2	Red	8 to 12oz	$1^1/_4$lb	24 or 22
3	–	12oz	$1^1/_2$lb	24 or 22
4	Green	1lb	$1^1/_2$lb	22 or 20
5	Blue	1 to $1^1/_2$lb	2lb	22 or 20
6	–	1 to $1^1/_2$lb	2lb	22 to 18
7	Black	$1^1/_2$ to $2^1/_2$lb	3lb	20 to 14
8	White	$1^1/_2$ to $2^1/_2$lb	3lb	20 to 14

To a lot of anglers the approach suggested by the table may seem very fine, certainly in the top half, but it needs to be if you are to get the best out of pole fishing. It is a precise and delicate way of fishing, and I always think of it as one step down from the equivalent job on the rod and reel. In a way the tackle is dictated by the strength of the elastic. The selection of hooks, hook lengths and main lines indicated in the table can be safely used with the recommended elastic, so why go any heavier? You will gain nothing by it, but will lose some of the finesse in both float control and bait presentation if you do step up.

What makes of line? It's a question I am always being asked, and the first answer is that I do not think anglers have ever been better served by line manufacturers. There's a lot of good stuff about, and whilst it might be unfair to some of them to mention brand names I do have personal preferences. I have also arrived at them without being influenced by any commercial ties or interests. The table deals in round figures, really. Where it says $1^1/_2$lbs I will actually be using 1.7lb Bayer, and for 1lb read 1.1lb Bayer. I much prefer Force when it comes to 8oz and 12oz hook lengths, but don't like this make at anything over 1lb. When it comes to the stronger lines of 2 to 3lbs, which I do not use all that often, I think there is a case for considering Daiwa's Harrier line, or the relatively new low-diameter, low stretch lines from Ultima. Being thin it isn't influenced by the wind as much as standard lines of the same breaking strain, and lack of stretch doesn't matter when a line is being used on an elastic set-up.

As for the hooks, virtually all the sizes mentioned in the table will be fine wire patterns with micro barbs. I don't use barbless with the pole, and rarely use forged hooks, which don't fit in with a finesse system. Carp are virtually the only species which have me reaching for forged hooks.

CHOOSING THE RIGHT FLOATS

by Tom Pickering

I often wonder which kind of fishing float was the first ever to be manufactured and sold in tackle shops. One of the quill types, possibly, but whatever it was it certainly started something. Millions of floats have been made ever since, many of them intended to catch anglers, rather than fish. Since the pole revolution began we have seen some of that repeated, though to be fair we don't see too many completely bad pole floats. One reason, of course, is that when we adopted the pole as a match fishing system we inherited a century or so of technology to go with it. We had already seen which types of float were employed by the continentals for a variety of different jobs, and mostly we took it from there. We imported their floats, especially from Italy and France, and some of our own float firms got into the act as well.

The reason for that preamble is to make the point that with many different companies in the game it is perhaps not surprising that there are lots of different float patterns, many of them varying only slightly. Beginners to the game go into a tackle shop and view the serried ranks of floats with total despair. One of my customers reckoned that my shop counter looked like a reconstruction of the Battle of Waterloo, and it was easy to see what he meant. Just like Waterloo, there were winners and losers on display, but with the pole the "loser" is likely to be a float chosen for the wrong job. It may be perfectly OK for some other purpose.

The best way for me to help you to sort out what is required is to give a guide to the basic shapes, and the jobs they are expected to do. We have pictures here which illustrate them, and I have arranged them in "family" groups. I shall select one or two from each family to discuss in a bit more detail, but the general advice, both here and elsewhere, will apply to any float you might want to use from that group. From this point in the book, wherever a shotting diagram is shown I will give the float the appropriate code letter and its overall loading, so you will know exactly what kind of float is required if you want to make the same tackle yourself. I will begin with Group A, the round-bodied floats (pictured next page). They come in a variety of different shapes and sizes (up to 3 grammes) and are designed to cope with virtually all the conditions we meet on running water. As you will see from the picture they are not all perfectly round

GROUP A

Just a few samples from the range of round-topped or round-bodied river floats we have classified as Group A

in the body, but they are all round shaped at the top of the body. This ensures that they all fish in more or less the same way.

Providing they are properly shotted they work well, and by properly shotted I do not simply mean the way the weight is distributed on the line. A correctly shotted pole float must have the whole of the body under water. It has to be shotted right onto the bristle. The key to the pole method is sensitivity, but if you have a bit of the float body poking above the surface you lose sensitivity. With an under-shotted pole float you are almost fishing the same way as you are with a stick float or a waggler. A guide to how to shot up properly is included in the next section of the book, but for now let's assume the round float is rigged correctly.

I most often use the Group A type with the perfectly round body, because I seem to get on very well with it. This shape, fully submerged, offers quite a large surface area for flowing water to push down on. That ensures that when the float is under close control it will not lift up in the water. If it does rise up when checked it is too small for the speed of flow, and you need more weight on - a subject I go into in more detail in the Techniques and Tactics chapter. If it is fishing properly, though, a biting fish only has to take that slender bristle

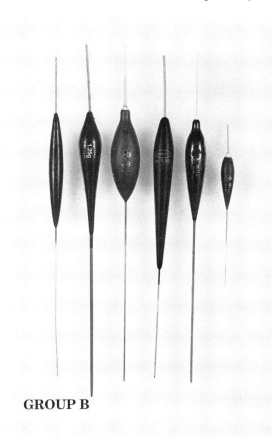

GROUP B

For rivers with slower flows, similar but slimmer floats are required, classified here as Group B

under, and it's as good as hooked. The next type of float, Group B, may not seem, at first sight, to be all that different, but as you will see from the pictures it has a more oval shape to the body, and it is one of several I use as a compromise float. Whilst that Group A round float is fine for many running water conditions it becomes a bit crude for slower flows. I use a Group B float for the deeper, steadier swims on the Trent at places like Long Higgin. There is still enough surface area for the float to hold down, but the more elongated shape of the body gives more sensitivity. It also works well on waters which can hold still and then move, like some canals and rivers with some tidal influence, like the Witham.

The round-bodied and oval shaped floats, however, are not suitable for stillwater or canal fishing, partly because the bodies would ride too near the surface. In choppy conditions, in particular, they will bob up and down with the waves, and we really want something more stable. That basically means a body shape or shapes which are more elongated, like those in the Group C picture. As you can see they have more of their bulk lower down in the water, and become progressively thinner towards the surface. It is more pronounced in some than in others as you can see from the picture, and there are good reasons for the differences.

The type with the shorter and fatter body is mainly used with a cane stem, and I like this one for the more perfect conditions on lakes and canals, especially for fishing on the drop. The cane stem helps to achieve a nice, slow cocking of the float, very much in tune with the falling of the shots and bait. It is very much like the presentation we have to achieve when stick float fishing. I particularly like using it for far bank work on canals, when the conditions permit, but it does a similar job, at any chosen distance, on lakes.

When conditions are rougher, though, this float starts to fail for the same reasons as the round float would. Even the elongated shape of body is now too close to the top, so we have to switch to the other type. The body is longer still and slower in the taper, which takes the thickest part of the body deeper down in the water. It also has a wire stem and that, combined with the body shape, gives us a much more stable float for windy weather. There are a great many floats in the Group C category, but they all have to be used on the lines

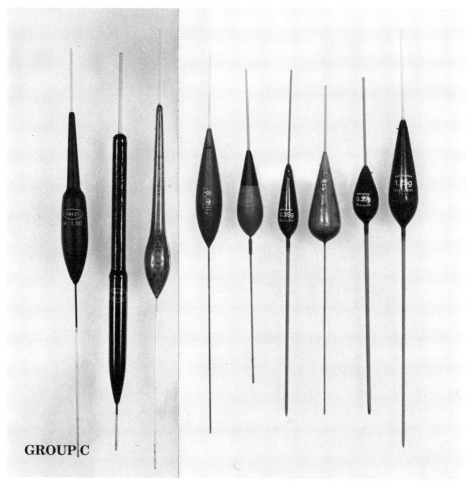

GROUP C

For still water and canal fishing the design of float changes yet again. You will require something from the Group C range.

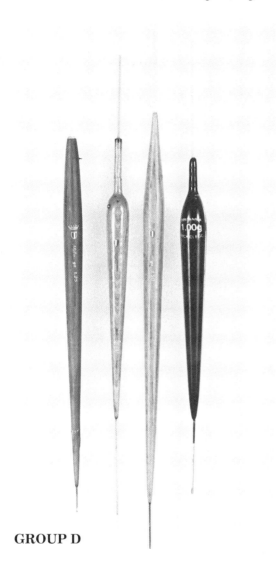

GROUP D

These are the all-balsa wood floats for bloodworm fishing, classified as Group D.

suggested here - cane stemmed for good conditions and for catching on the drop; wire-stemmed, slimmer and more elongated for windier conditions and for catching on or closer to the bottom.

Group D floats require very little explanation at this stage. They are the ones I use for bloodworm fishing on stillwaters and canals. The elongated bodies are all balsa, and they are obviously made to take a bit of weight. Virtually all the time they are used with olivettes and one or two dropper shots, as described later on.

When conditions are too rough for the use of any type of float attached top and bottom we have to resort to Group E floats (pictured overleaf). These are the smaller end of the waggler float range, mostly made for rod and reel fishing.

They are, however, vital for the pole man in a series of circumstances dealt with later on. I favour crystal wagglers for most of the situations requiring the use of floats attached bottom only, mostly because they have a very slim and sensitive insert in the tips. Canal Greys and one or two other types will do the job as well.

So there we have a vast selection of floats categorised into five separate families. They all have different uses, and in one size or another will cope with just about every kind of situation we are likely to encounter in pole fishing. Keep the five groups in mind when you are confronted in the tackle shop with all manner of variations. Now you know what the basic shapes are used for you are able to sort out what you need for the particular waters where you use the pole. I will, of course, be detailing exactly how these floats are used a little later, together with suitable shotting diagrams.

GROUP E

Group E, the small crystal wagglers.

SHOTTING FLOATS AT HOME

by Tom Pickering

In our early days of pole fishing it was considered necessary to make up all our pole tackles at home, partly because it was a fiddly job demanding great precision. I think some people overdo this job a bit, and they need a box like a tea chest to store all their tackles and the winders. I confine myself to just a few home-made rigs for waters I fish on a regular basis. If I find I want something different for a new water, or somewhere I do not fish all that often, I will make one on the spot. It doesn't take all that long.

Originally we were working with floats which did not have the overall weight carrying capacity on them, and we also thought that every pole rig had to have the appropriate olivette or similar weight, plus one or two droppers. We had to experiment to find the right olivette, and then add tiny micro shot to get the float shotted onto the bristle. We have come to learn, however, that for the vast majority of occasions we are better off with similar shotting patterns to those we use for other forms of float fishing, but slightly miniaturised, sometimes.

Simple shotting jobs are easily done on the bank, especially when you are simply practising, and then you just save the resulting, properly adjusted rig for the next visit, possibly making a duplicate rig at home later on. It is very much easier to work at home now, thanks to the arrival of possibly the most useful of all the pole fishing accessories - the Dosapiombo. As you can perhaps gather from the pictures overleaf, the "Dossy" is a neutral buoyancy device. Jam the bottom end of a pole float into the hole provided, trap it in place by adjusting the little lever and drop it into your test tank. All you have to do now is add the appropriate weights to the "platform" at the top of the "Dossy" until the float settles to the correct position - i.e. with the whole of the float body under water and part of the bristle under as well.

The better floats now have number codes to indicate the overall weight carrying capacity. They are fairly accurate, but they are all made to size with balsa, as a rule, and this wood can vary in character quite a bit. The codes are rarely 100 per cent accurate, but they are still very useful guides. I have produced a table (page 35) which will help you to de-code the float markings. It gives the olivette size and, where relevant, the alternative round shot or styl lead capacities.

Using the table for, say, a float marked .25, you would choose a size 1 olivette, and there should be enough capacity left for two or three dropper shots. If you require a shotting pattern for the same float it would be based on six no. 10

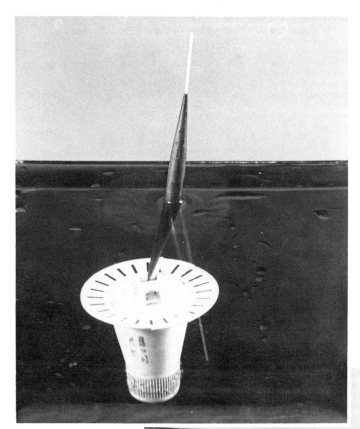

How to use the Dosapiombo. Here the float has been clipped into the neutral buoyancy device and is ready for the shotting exercise.

Add shots to the platform until the float sinks down to, and onto, the bristle. In this example, just one more small shot would do the trick. Put the float and shots on a tackle and it should be perfect.

34

CRACKING THE FLOAT CODES

Float marking:	.10	.15	.20	.25	.30	.40	.50	.75
Olivette	–	–	–	1	–	2	3	4
Shot	3x10	4x10	5x10	6x10	4x8	6x8	5x6	6x6
Styl	4x9	4x11	4x12	4x13	3x14	4x14	4x16	4x18

Float marking:	1gr	1.25	1.50	2gr	2.50	3gr		
Olivette	5	6	7	8	9	10		
Shot	5x4	6x4	7x4	–	5BB	4AA		
Styl	6x18	4x20	5x20	–	–	–		

(IMPORTANT FOOTNOTE: Lead shot above size 8 is now illegal, so use substitutes. Styl leads of size 13 and over are also illegal, and there are no substitutes. You can make up with legal sizes or a mix of Styl and round weights).

shots, or an 8 and some 10s. With Styl leads (mentioned in more detail at the end of this chapter) you would need four no. 13s. Whatever type of rig you need, just load up the "Dossy" until you get the right register on the float. Then you can safely arrange the weights on the line, under the float, put it on a winder, and it will be perfect when it goes into action. It's a vast improvement on the system we had before the "Dossy" came along. We had to hang some line from a float, add all the required weights to that and then take them all off again, putting them back onto the tackle proper. Half the time we couldn't open the shots we had pinched on the test line, and we had to find a similarly sized shot which, sometimes, would be just a fraction lighter or heavier. It was a messy, time-consuming business requiring a lot of patience.

The "Dossy" system is a doddle in comparison, but those who have used it will realise that I have slightly over-simplified the description of how it is used, especially with the smaller and more delicate floats. Getting them shotted onto the bristle can be difficult. You get to the point where the top of the body is just about level with the water. Then you add one little shot to the "Dossy"... and it all sinks slowly out of sight! You have overdone it, and getting it dead right can be a real pig of a job. How's it done? Don't bother. A float which sinks very slowly out of sight, or clings to the surface with little or nothing of the bristle showing, can be "doctored" when you are fishing with it.

The trick is so simple. I carry a tin of Mucilin grease, which the fly anglers use to make their leaders float, and which pike men coat their lines with for drift float fishing. Just poke the pole float bristle into it for the required distance, and then withdraw it. That over-shotted float will now sit proudly above the surface for the length of bristle you have greased. If it eventually starts to sink, just grease it again. How much

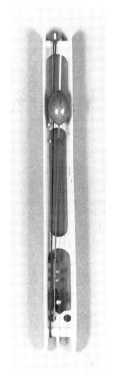

Completed float tackle on a winder.

more sensitive can you get? A float which is held up by a minute coating of grease, compensating for a fraction of over-shotting, has to be the most delicate form of presentation yet devised. It's almost unfair on the fish!

I got onto the grease dodge via fellow England international Bob Nudd, while I was really looking for an answer to another difficulty I had to overcome. Unlike quite a few of the leading pole anglers I like to use pole floats which have removable, and therefore interchangeable, bristles. The one problem with them is that if the bristle is not a perfect fit water can get into the float body and ruin it, but it can be solved by using the same greasing tactic. When a greased bristle is pushed home into the float body it is perfectly waterproofed for as long as that bristle is in place. You obviously repeat the exercise when you change the bristle.

Why change a bristle at all? One reason is that I sometimes like a longer bristle, up to 2", than the one which comes with the float. It gets the float body that bit further under the surface in windy conditions. It is also handy to be able to change the colour of the bristle for different light conditions. Fishing in sky reflection you will probably find that black is the easiest colour to see. Against tree shadow you need a colour - orange, yellow or red. If you don't have interchangeable bristles you need at least two identical rigs, or you have to carry some quick drying paint. I think it is easier to change the bristles or, failing that, to have all your bristles one colour, say orange, and carry a felt-tipped pen to change them to black, when required. Another good idea which Silstar Goldthorpe angler Bob Roberts came up with in a recent feature in Coarse Angler magazine, is to have reversible bristles painted half black, half orange.

Having got myself side-tracked with grease and bristle technology, let's get back to tackling up at home. One obvious point to make is that you must know a good bit about the water you are making the tackle for. You have to keep in mind the main species and average size of fish present, and the approximate depth at the range you intend to fish. If you have that information, and you have sorted out the right float and got the shotting capacity worked out with the "Dossy", you are ready to put the tackle together. For relevant line strengths and hook sizes, refer to the table in the chapter about elastics.

As we shall see later on, the length of line between pole tip and float can vary a good bit, according to the kind of fishing being done. You will have to adjust the information in this chapter in the light of what you learn later, but for now I will deal with the making of just one type of pole rig, a tackle for a stillwater which is about two metres deep. For most stillwater situations I like to have the float no more than 2ft from the tip of the pole, so we are talking about an overall length of tackle of a little less than three metres. With that you are able to fish to hand with three metres of pole, or add sections if you want to fish further out. The tackle, though, is tailored to three metres, so the first step is to assemble that length of the pole. Tie a loop in the end of the chosen main line, using a similar knot (Fig 9) to the

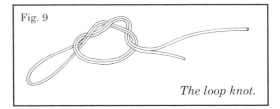

Fig. 9

The loop knot.

one described for the elastic in a previous chapter. A quick reminder: double the end of the line back on itself, make a circle with the doubled end and pass the end through the circle. This time, though, take the end through twice, and tighten. Put the resulting loop into the hook on the Stonfo at the end of the pole, and slide the cap over the hook to hold it in place.

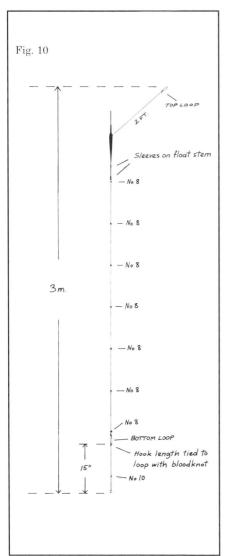

Fig. 10

The make-up of a standard tackle.

Run off a length of line of almost the full length of the pole and put the float on via the top eye. It has to be fastened with tight-fitting plastic sleeves pushed onto the wire or cane stem - probably cane, in this particular case. One sleeve pushes right up to the underside of the float body with the other and slightly longer piece at the base of the cane and overhanging the line. It is best to take the float up to a position 2ft from the end of the pole before fitting the sleeves. It isn't a good idea to fasten it at the bottom end of the line and push the float all the way up to the correct position, for that could generate friction which might weaken the line.

The next job is to repeat the loop at the bottom end of the line, using the knot just described, only this time make the final loop as small as possible, to minimise the possibility of tackle tangles when the rig is used. You have to tie that loop in exactly the right place, bearing in mind that there is a hook length of approximately 15" to add later. The overall length has to be a little over 2 metres to the float including the hook length, with that further 2ft. above the float. All you have to do now is pinch the shots on. In this example (Fig 10) you have a few number 8s evenly spaced, with a No. 10 nearest the hook.

Many anglers like to have a short hook length with no shot on it, because they think a shot can weaken the hook length. I don't agree with them, mainly because I like a longer length of line to the hook. It's less "rigid," or more supple, if you like. I think it helps to present a bait with a more natural fall, but of course it requires a terminal shot nearer the hook than 15 inches. If that shot is carefully nipped on it should cause no problems.

For various reasons I do not put hooks onto pole tackles I make at home. Once the main line is all rigged up I put it on a winder, always using a winder longer

37

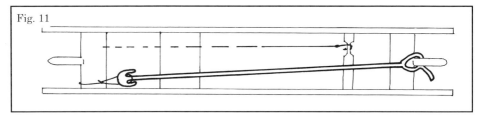

After winding on the tackle (greatly simplified in this drawing!) an elasticated anchor is invaluable to finish off the job.

than the float. If you have a float overlapping a winder it is prone to breakage. I put the loop at the bottom (the one which will be nearest the hook) on the winder spike and wrap the tackle round and round until I reach the other loop. I connect that to the spike with an elastic anchor (Fig 11) - another invaluable accessory for the pole angler.

Not putting a hook length on means I have to shot the float up as described, and then subtract the terminal no. 10 (or sometimes a 12), and add it back to the chosen hook length later, which is no problem. This system is more flexible. It gives you a choice of hook size and breaking strain of hook length. I carry a variety of ready tied hooks on 18" lengths of line. I use them for all kinds of fishing, waggler, stick float, legering or whatever. When I want to pick up the pole I just adapt an appropriate hook length to 15" (sometimes less) on the pole tackle.

How is it attached to the pole tackle? Some anglers tie yet another loop to the hook length and link them together, but I'm not too happy with that. Specialist anglers have shown that the loop knot does not have a high knot strength. It doesn't matter when you are using it on the stronger of two lengths of line, but I think it does on the weaker link. Two loops together are also untidy and tangle prone, so I attach my hook lengths to the loop with a carefully tied half blood knot (Fig 12), wetting it with my mouth before snugging it up tight. The half blood is a stronger knot, and truth be told I would like to attach hook length and main line with a full blood knot. Unfortunately it isn't practicable, for if I subsequently break the hook length on a snag there is no way of tying on a new one without losing the depth. Precision with the depth setting is vital, as we shall see later, and we don't want to be re-plumbing all the time. With any pole tackle, therefore, you need one small shot directly under the float. It can be a few inches below the float on the winder, but once the exact depth has been plumbed it must be moved directly under the float as a depth marker.

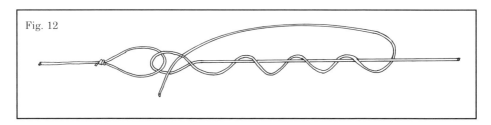

The half bloodknot for attaching hooklengths to the bottom loop.

RIGGING UP WITH OLIVETTES

This subject should be covered under the general heading of rigging up at home. With shots were are mostly dealing with legal sizes of lead shot (size 8 and smaller), plus size 6 and sometimes 4 shots made from non-toxic materials. When the swan lead poisoning problem led to the banning of all lead weights between 8s and 1oz we thought we were in trouble with olivette style pole fishing, but the reverse proved to be the case. We ended up with a substitute which was even better than the original - the tungsten Streamline weights, which have just about cornered the market.

They are actually smaller than lead olivettes of the same weight, and therefore sink faster - an advantage, because when we are fishing with these weights we are wanting to get down fast to fish feeding on or near the bottom. The one drawback is that the central holes in these weights are (a) too big in diameter and (b) a bit rough, which can cause eventual wear and breakage of the main line. We solved both problems by fitting them up with internal plastic or rubber pole float sleeves, slightly protruding from either end of the weight. Many anglers, knowing of the solution, have driven themselves crazy trying to get sleeving through the hole! I shall now put them out of their misery. It is very easy, when you know how.

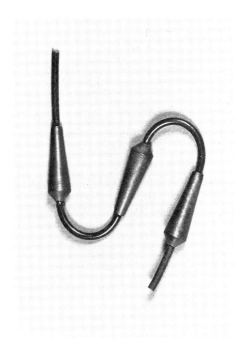

Streamline olivettes threaded onto tubing. Cut them off as required, leaving a bit of tubing standing proud at both ends.

You can buy pole float sleeves cut to length, but you want the sort which comes in uncut lengths of several inches. Yes, I know, it doesn't go through either, but it will in a few seconds! Hold one end of the sleeving with thumb and forefinger, and grip with the other hand about an inch away. Pass the sleeving over a lighted candle and swiftly pull apart as the plastic melts. You will now have a length of sleeving with a long, thin "spike" on the end. That will pass through a Streamline weight. In fact you should thread several weights up the plastic until the length runs out, and cut them off with scissors or a craftsman's knife.

Streamline weights are sold, now, with a length of material which is intended for use as internal sleeving. At one time this would also respond to the candle treatment, but the last time I tried it, it didn't. Unfortunately it looks as though they have changed it, but a young man in my shop sorted out a way. He passed a loop of strong line through one of the weights, put the sleeving through the loop and pulled it through doubled. So, whatever the material, there are now at least two ways to do the job.

These weights are invariably fixed well down the line, about 2ft from the hook and stopped in place by two small shots, usually no. 8s, placed together. Between those weights and hook there will be only one other shot. The reasons for this arrangement are covered in more detail later.

STYL LEADS

It is not often that I will avoid using something I consider to be superior to anything else, but Styl leads are the exception. I think they are a splendid concept, and that they offer a rather better way of fishing with some methods than the more conventional system using round shot. They are particularly good for fishing on the drop, a method I use a great deal, as you will see. For those not familiar with Styls, they are cylindrical weights with the split running lengthways. They are made with great precision, in good quality soft lead, and they are legal for use in this country in sizes up to and including 12.

They were originally available in two dispensers, with each size in a separate compartment. Luckily for us it's the one with the smaller sizes in it which remains legal, but it's a great pity we lost the other Styl weights. I never saw any evidence that Styls were poisoning swans. We never lost them, and Styl tackles were almost invariably retained for re-use. However, that's water under the bridge now. The appropriate legal sizes are shaken into the centre of the container, or some other flat surface, where they have to be

Dispenser containing the legal sizes of Styl weights.

picked up with special Styl pliers. Select a weight which has the split face down, taking care to get the full length of the lead flush with the front edge of the pliers. You squeeze just hard enough to pick it up, then place the line along the split with the free hand. Gently apply just enough pressure to fix the weight on the line without damaging it (Fig 13).

It is the fiddly method of attachment which, more than anything, persuades me not to use them all that often. The job is best done on tackles made at home, and as I have already said I make most of mine on the bank. Anglers who do use

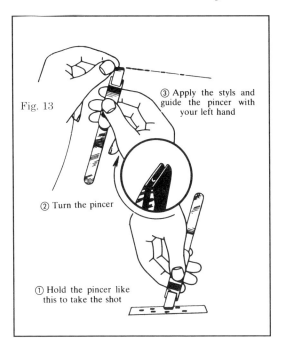

Fig. 13

③ Apply the styls and guide the pincer with your left hand

② Turn the pincer

① Hold the pincer like this to take the shot

How Styl weights are attached with special pincers (drawing from supplier's leaflet).

Styls a great deal acquire the skill to do the job quickly, whether at home or while fishing. In doing so they certainly acquire a marginal edge over those who do not bother, and I do not knock that at all. Some anglers take a great deal of pride in their tackles, and it probably gives them the confidence to fish better.

I weigh the disadvantages - or what I see as disadvantages - against the plus points. For me it is a longer job than nipping on a shot, and while the pliers will mostly put them on firmly, but still movable, the odd one tends to hold fast. You will come to realise that the ability to move weights from strung out to bunched, and possibly back again later, is a vital necessity in pole fishing. If I put two Styls on properly, and then I get one which sticks, the tackle is no good to me. It has to be instantly variable, so I have to start again. The other big minus is when a Styl comes off. It can happen if a fish brushes the line against something when I am playing it, or sometimes when I am moving it. I then have to sort out which size of weight I have lost, and the sizes are too close to each other to be easily recognisable. Noting the numbers down on the side of the pole winder would be the best way out of that problem.

It is certainly a good idea to code mark winders with information which assists correct choice on the bankside, for it is surprising how quickly you can forget. Something like SK 8 8 8 10 would remind me that it's a Stainforth & Keadby Canal tackle, and not a three 8s and a 10 rig I made for a more shallow canal. I would not need to remind myself what line it's on, but others might. It certainly does no harm to be efficient and properly organised, but I have chosen not to be so organised when it comes to Styl leads.

Do not let me put you off, though. For those who are prepared to take the trouble Styl leads are great, and if I fished a smaller variety of waters I would probably use them far more often than I do at the moment.

Before leaving the subject of tackle making it is perhaps the right moment to advise on the ideal size of float to choose for a variety of different waters. You have been told how the floats split up into family groups for different types of fishing in various conditions. The previous table in this section broke down the code markings on those floats into olivette, shot and Styl weight capacities. The one which follows will suggest which code number to select for particular types of water. Clearly I can only make suggestions for waters I fish, but I have tried to make my list representative of the fishing generally available - fast and slow rivers, a couple of stillwaters and a variety of canals. The table mostly assumes perfect conditions, so do not be afraid to step up from these sizes if you have to.

WHICH SIZE OF FLOAT?

	Maggot Fishing		Bloodworm Fishing	
	<u>Olivette</u>	<u>Shot/Styl</u>	<u>Olivette</u>	<u>Shot/Styl</u>
River Trent	–	.75 to 1.50	–	–
Tidal Trent	1.50 to 3.00	–	–	–
River Witham	–	.50 normal .75 windy 1.0 running	.50 normal 1.0 running	– –
M. Weighton Canal	–	.50	.50	–
Welland/Coronation	–	.50	.50	–
Stainforth Canal	–	.30 .60 windy	.15 –	 .30 windy
New Junction Canal	1.0	–	–	–
Bridgewater Canal	–	.15	–	.15
Grand Union Canal	–	.15	–	.15
Leeds/Liverpool Canal	–	.50 (gudgeon)	–	.30 .50 (gudgeon)
Worsborough Reservoir	–	.30 shallows/roach 1.0 deeps	–	–
River Soar	–	.30 to .50	–	.30
Warwickshire Avon	–	.50 shallow .75 deeper	.50	–
River Nene	–	.50 shallow .75 deeps	.75	–
Rudyard Lake	1.0	.50 shallow	–	–

PLUMBING THE DEPTHS

by Tom Pickering

Knowing the exact depth of a swim is essential in any form of fishing, but for the pole it is particularly important. Luckily plumbing is an easier job with the pole than it is when rod and reel fishing. In fact there is a good case for using a pole to find the depth, even if you actually intend to fish the stick float or even the waggler, inside the limit of a pole length. Plumbing is a job many anglers either don't do at all or don't do properly, and I will admit to learning something about it only recently, from a feature article Bob Roberts did for Coarse Angler magazine.

He advocated plumbing a bit further out than you intend to fish, finding the exact depth with a heavy plummet. Lowering the weight carefully, and adjusting the float so that the tip shows just above the surface, is just routine, but more often than not Bob's method requires that job to be done only once. When he finds the depth well out all he does then is to plumb back towards the bank, noting where the depth changes simply by looking at how far the float is showing above the water (see Fig 14 overleaf). In the vast majority of swims, on rivers or stillwaters, the water will get more shallow closer in, and his method will reveal exactly where the near shelf is (if there is one). If there is more than one shelf it will show that, too, and it will also tell you if there is a deeper gulley between you and the end of the pole. The float will simply disappear into it when it reaches that point. The system accurately reveals the whole contour between you and the limits of your pole.

Reading that made me wonder how many anglers had not actually tumbled to that way of doing it. We all learned our plumbing with rods and reels, working slowly outwards from the bank and adjusting the float umpteen times. With wagglers on flowing water anglers really have to struggle, usually putting a big shot on the hook and slowly deepening the float until the shot causes the float to pull under when it drags bottom. Rod and reel plumbing is not easy, but with the pole - especially using Bob Roberts' method - there are no problems at all.

We are not limited by a relatively short rod, and when we have worked out the contour in a straight line in front of us we can then move the pole all around the area we have decided to fish, to see if there are any slight or even big depth changes. It can be a mistake to assume that the depth below the pole tip, directly

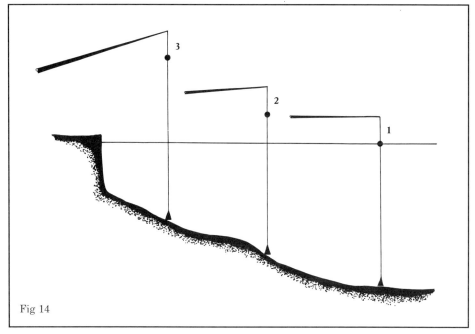

Fig 14

The best way to plumb the depth with the pole is to start well out and move back towards the bank.

to the front, is the depth of the whole area. You might have lowered the plummet onto the top of a hump, and any fish would possibly be around the sides or the bottom of that hump. On a river knowing whether the depth changes downstream is a big advantage. It is no use setting up to fish six feet if the swim is seven feet deep a yard or so further down - or five feet, for that matter. Depth variations dictate how effectively we can fish, and how we fish, in some cases.

Finding gulleys and shelves is important, simply because they are fish-holding areas. It is usually better to fish a shelf at, say, 8 metres than a flat and featureless area three or four metres further out, though the smart pole angler will usually opt to feed both areas, and switch around between the two. It's interesting looking at the graph readings which some specialist anglers are now getting from sonar equipment. Colin Dyson showed me some where there were no fish at all for great distances on flat bottoms. Suddenly there would be a single fish or a shoal of fish where the depth changed, sometimes only slightly. It is entirely consistent with what we find as match anglers. Swims with some sort of feature in them, including snags, if it is possible to fish near them without snagging the tackle, are generally better than those with no character. If there is no fishable feature, however, it pays to fish as far out as possible and attract fish in with the feed.

Wherever we decide to fish, after careful plumbing, the main decision remaining is whether to fish the exact depth, a little off the bottom or with some line on the bottom. That depends mainly on what we are fishing for, and it is covered under various headings elsewhere.

POLE HANDLING TECHNIQUES

by Tom Pickering

This subject is going to be mostly dealt with photographically, with suitable captions. The aim, always, is to handle efficiently and comfortably, and I do not really believe that it has to be taught. Most anglers, confronted with the problem of handling a long pole, naturally adopt the most comfortable way of doing the job. A very strong man will find some things easier than someone of slighter build and less strength. But I am not exactly frightening the current Mr Universe. Colin Dyson reckons I could live inside a pole, and he isn't far

The standard method of holding a long pole while sitting down. It is supported along the thigh with the rear hand pushing down, and the forward hand ready to lift to hook a biting fish.

wrong! I do not, however, experience any great difficulty in handling poles, even at the extreme lengths. It may seem awkward at first, but the more you get into it the easier it is. My pictures are mere guidelines for you to either copy or to adapt to suit yourself. What is important is to realise that the overall aim is to handle the pole at all times in ways which will achieve efficiency. Be smooth, careful and gentle in whatever you do. When the float is out of the water the sole aim is not to jerk it around and tangle to tackle. The hook must not catch something it shouldn't, like bits of grass, bankside vegetation, your clothing or you! When it is in the water it must be fishing for you, and under control the whole time. Whoever called angling the gentle art was not kidding, and we are never more gentle and delicate than we are when pole fishing. Elsewhere in the book I go into detail about what we are attempting to achieve with the floats, but it is neat, precise pole handling which gets the results. Bear that in mind when you study the pictures, and the information relating to them.

Long shot of the same holding method demonstrated in the picture on the previous page.

An alternative posture, with the butt tucked into the crutch and both hands supporting the weight. This method gives a fraction more length, and gives you a bit of a rest.

The "crutch" method also offers a comfortable way of handling the pole

The same method also gives you this "hands-off" option, if you want to catapult loose feed or throw groundbait.

Tom Pickering's way of handling a short, or un-shipped pole. Crooking the little finger over it frees the important fingers of both hands for re-baiting the hook.

Here the writer is adding one of three spare sections. These must be kept in easy reach if you want to fish further out, or if big fish are expected (for the reasons why, see "Coping with Carp" chapter.)

48

The writer (top) has lifted his pole to strike a small fish, and (below) has started to feed the pole backwards, prior to unshipping at the appropriate length to land the fish. Note the use of the pole roller, which allows him to feed back without damaging the pole on the stones.

There is a right and wrong way to use a pole roller, and this is the wrong one. After unshipping to land his fish the writer is now having to turn and look for the pole and reach up in the air for it.

The correct way is to place the roller far enough back for the point of balance to remain between roller and angler. That way the un-shipped section stays down, and the front end holds in the tray on the side of the box, ready for rapid re-assembly.

Casting is mostly common-sense. How to lay the tackle out is described elsewhere, but here are the basics of getting the float to the required area with a long pole. Drop the float in the water with the short length of pole being fished to hand, and ship the full length being used. Then begin to feed the whole length forward, as seen here.

When the full length is out, raise the pole to lay the float tackle across the baited area, or drop the tackle straight onto the bait if using an olivette rig.

When the pole has been lowered after casting, the main tasks are to control the float, moving it to attract bites (as described elsewhere), or lifting and re-casting again at regular intervals if you are trying to catch on the drop.

Pole handling while standing up requires a little more physical effort, because there is no thigh support. The standard method is illustrated below.

Fishing with a pole section, or part of one, behind the hands, can help to balance the pole, but it is necessary when fishing rivers. The float is dropped in front of the angler, with the pole angled upstream, as above. The angler "follows" the float downstream with the tip of the pole, keeping it under close control. When it reaches the limit of its travel, the "spare" pole section can be fed forward to allow the float to cover more of the swim.

To free a hand for throwing bait the butt of the pole can be jammed into the pit of the stomach, as shown above.

TECHNIQUES & TACTICS

by Tom Pickering

STILLWATERS

One of the first things Britain's top anglers learned when pole fishing began to take off here was that the Continental method should not be slavishly copied. I saw their approach as interesting but incomplete. It was clear from all the early information gleaned from the French, in particular, that their approach was heavily geared to catching on or close to the bottom. Every shotting diagram which crossed the English Channel seemed to have an olivette weight in it, set somewhere close to the hook or not very far away. As we now know their system is geared to the way they feed their swims. Their aim, most of the time, is to get the fish feeding on the bottom and to get their baited hooks down to the fish as rapidly as possible.

That seemed OK to me as far as it went, but I could not see why they always wanted to dictate to the fish. Our match fishing approach up to that time had been developed to cope with whatever moods the fish were in on a given day. Catching them how they want to be caught is not a particularly accurate description, but it does sum it up. We had always tried to respond to the many different ways in which fish behave; to find out as quickly as possible how to catch as many as possible in a given time. That approach had served me well for years on the rod and reel, float and leger, and I wasn't about to throw it all overboard simply to follow a foreign fashion.

Instead I looked at the pole and tried to evaluate the advantages the method had to offer and how I could use those advantages to improve my own results. Clearly the pole could score in many situations where fish could be caught close in, and as poles got lighter and longer, of course, "close in" has got further out! Within the limits of pole length I set out to both duplicate and refine existing methods, using the Continental approach as an additional tactic.

With rare exceptions, like in bream fishing, for example, we don't use groundbait as often or as heavily as the continentals. We base our main approach on loose-feeding with maggot, caster, pinkie or squatt, and wait to see how the fish we are after respond to that feed. Many times the fish are either off the bottom to begin with or will come off bottom to intercept feed. When specialist anglers first started to play around with electronic fish-finding equipment they were surprised how often fish shoals were located way off bottom - even bream and eels, at times. Those who have used such equipment regularly are now concluding that fish spend most of their time off bottom. I smiled a bit when I read about it, for I had been cashing in on that knowledge for years. If I was to work out how much of my match winnings had been earned catching fish off the bottom I would be surprised if it didn't come to somewhere between 60 and 75 per cent.

If fish are off the bottom so often it makes little sense to start fishing for them on the bottom. Instead we should be searching the full depth, from surface to bottom, and responding to what happens. I mentioned one example of stillwater fishing earlier, when discussing the make-up of pole tackles. Now is the time to take it a bit further. A correct stillwater rig will have one of the floats with an elongated body, a bristle and either a wire or cane stem - preferably the latter, if we can get away with it. There will be no more than 2ft of line from pole tip to float, and below the float will be just enough line for the hook to reach bottom, perhaps a few inches over depth. If you are making a tackle on the bank it pays to err on the long side to begin with, and adjust the distance from float to pole after the depth has been accurately plumbed. As I said in the earlier chapter, you should only make up tackles at home if you know the nature of the swims you are making the tackle for. If depths vary on a given water, then you obviously make them up for the deepest sections, and shorten if you need to.

Once the tackle length has been ascertained the key job is the shotting, and that obviously varies with the depth. For shallow swims I will string out a couple of 8s and a 10 nearest the hook. The number and sometimes the size of shots increases with the depth, and obviously float size increases with it. It isn't necessary to cover every single shotting pattern I use, For they are all basically the same. They all have two things in common - the shots are always evenly spaced out at the start, from a depth marker shot under the float to a small dropper shot near the hook, usually a 10, sometimes an 8 or a 12. Possibly the most common approach I use is a float taking three no. 6 shot, an 8 and a 10 for water about 5 to 6ft deep (Fig 15). For

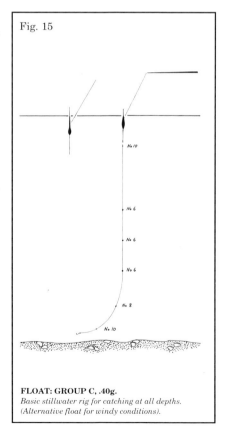

Fig. 15

FLOAT: GROUP C, .40g.
Basic stillwater rig for catching at all depths.
(Alternative float for windy conditions).

every foot deeper there would be another no. 6, with perhaps one or two no. 4 shots being introduced at the upper end on the occasional water which is very deep within pole range.

Mainly, I suppose, we are after roach and skimmer bream, and both species can be taken off bottom. The float is set to fish the full depth, but with even shotting, tapering down in size, we achieve a nice slow fall of the baited hook. It is going down with the feed in a natural manner, and it can be taken anywhere, from a foot below the surface to the bottom. You have to watch and learn how long it takes for the float to settle after a proper cast - and that means manipulating the pole to lay the tackle on the water in a straight line (Fig 16).

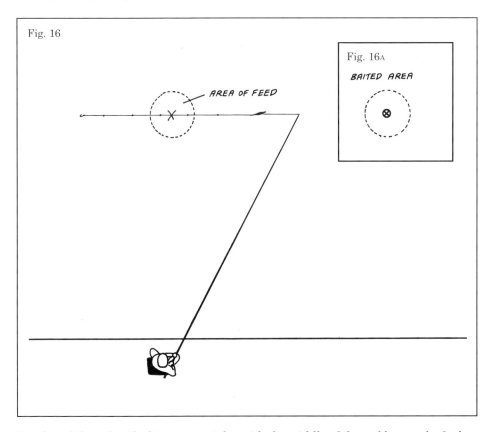

For drop fishing lay the line out straight, with the middle of the tackle over the feed area. As the tackle sinks the float will be drawn right into the baited area. When using an olivette, or any other rig designed to catch on the bottom, lower the tackle straight down the "hole" (Fig. 16A).

That way you will achieve that nice, slow fall. If you drop it in a heap it will go down both fast and untidily (though lowering straight down, see 16a, is desirable when using olivette rigs). Just hold the pole above the baited area, with all the tackle out of the water. Swing it one way to get the tackle moving from the vertical towards horizontal, then take the pole in the opposite direction and lower it at the same time. It's a smooth operation which takes a lot less time to actually do than it takes to describe. Try to place the tackle so that it lays across the baited area. Once you have done that move the pole towards the float to create a bit of slack line, and watch the float as the tackle sinks.

It will be pulled into the middle of the baited area as the shots sink, and you will also see it begin to cock as each individual shot sinks to its depth, finally settling down onto the bristle as the terminal number 10 finally registers. You are trying to establish how the float normally behaves, and if there is any delay in a shot registering, or the float moves sideways, or anything else unusual happens, you have a bite on the drop. If it all settles normally you then watch for a bite from fish on or very near the bottom, which will be signalled by a lift on the bristle or a sudden disappearance of the float. With this approach you are fishing the whole depth, searching the water in a thorough way, but it is by no means the end of the story.

Hopefully your steady loose feed will build up the swim, and you will start to get more bites. The task now is to note the depth at which the majority of the bites are coming. If they are all coming high in the water carry on with what you are doing, lifting the tackle out as soon as you think the bait has gone through the fish and laying it out on top again, as previously described. But you may find, instead, that all the bites are coming in the bottom half. If that happens you should then move all the shots at the top end of the tackle down to join the one in the middle (Fig 17). That takes the tackle down faster to the productive depth, but with the rest of the shots strung out as before the bait presentation will still be perfect where it counts.

We still haven't exhausted all the possibilities, though. When the fish are taking the bait in the bottom half, but no bites are coming when the hook actually reaches bottom, it can then pay to shorten the tackle by lowering the float a few inches. Quite often the fish will take the bait as it drops and then holds, right in front of their noses, and if they stay at that depth for any length of time you will put a good catch together.

The response, if most or all of the bites are coming on or near the bottom is to bunch all the shot together except the last two, to get down quickly. That's as near as I get to the olivette method on stillwaters. If you have a spare pole it might pay to have a pole with olivette and dropper shot rigged up, for there is no doubt that this will go down faster still, but I don't often bother. I would rather persevere with the system I am fishing to, and there is one inescapable fact to take into account - you cannot split up an olivette! You can re-arrange a bunch of shot, and there are times when you might have to put the sequence of events I have just described into reverse. The fish may be on the bottom because they aren't all that interested at first, but they can lift up later if the loose feeding switches them on. If bites slow down or stop on the bottom I will revert to a bunch of shot at half depth, to try and catch in the bottom half, or string them all out as they were originally to find out if the fish are now in the top half.

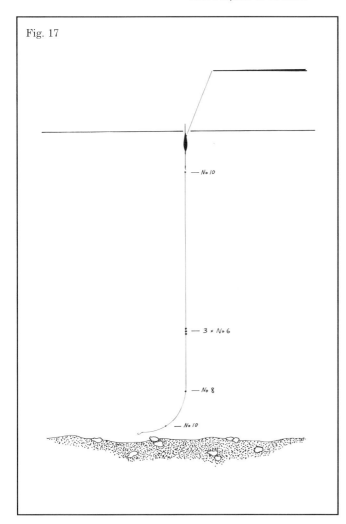

Fig. 17

— No 10

— 3 × No 6

— No 8

— No 10

FLOAT:
GROUP C, .40g.
A stillwater tackle
which is designed to
catch fish in the
bottom half.

It is not a lazy way of fishing. It is busy, especially when you are catching on the drop. You are lifting up and re-laying it all the time, and it is a faster and more effective way of fishing than is possible with rod and reel. It is also more accurate and vastly more sensitive. Only if all the bites are coming on the bottom do we sit and wait a bit, but even then it can pay to work the bait, lifting it and moving a bit in an attempt to provoke a bite. If you miss a bite you can leave the bait in the same place for a while, whereas with rod and reel the missed strike will have taken the hookbait out of the baited area. It has to be reeled in and re-cast. Taking into account all the other advantages, not least the smaller float and the sensitive bristle, the pole is unbeatable on a stillwater at distances up to about 14 metres.

One further point I ought to make about presentation is that when you are fishing a bunch of shot or an olivette you don't need to lay the tackle out straight. Just lower it straight down - it's quicker.

CANALS AND SLOW RIVERS

Much of the advice just given for stillwaters also applies to some of the deeper canals, which sometimes have a bit of movement, and also to some slow rivers - the Warwickshire Avon, for example, the River Witham and some parts of the Trent. Fishing moving water requires a different approach in some circumstances, including a longer length of line between the float and the pole tip. This helps you to run a float through the swim, if you want to, but I shall be covering that aspect of it a little later on.

For now I will continue on the method of catching on the drop, which is just as relevant to rivers as it is for stillwaters. Once again we need shotting patterns rather than olivettes, for all the same reasons described for stillwaters. River fish generally behave in exactly the same way, so they need the same basic approach - probably using some of the bigger floats in the stillwater range, given reasonable conditions. There is an example of the standard rig here (Fig 18). Tactics depend to some extent on the behaviour patterns of the fish in different waters, of course, so you may have to add or subtract little bits from the usual repertoire of "tricks."

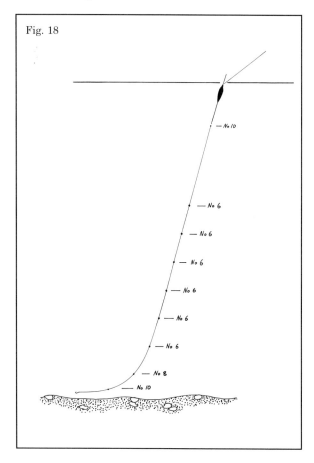

Fig. 18

— No 10

— No 6
— No 6
— No 6
— No 6
— No 6
— No 6
— No 8
— No 10

FLOAT:
GROUP B, .75g.
A river rig for catching on the drop.

60

On the River Witham, for example, I use the basic stillwater approach, but I often find there that a lot of my drop bites are coming in the very last foot of the depth. When I know my bait has gone through to the bottom, therefore, I will lift the pole about a foot and drop it back in (Fig 19). It is amazing how many times that movement will provoke an instant bite from a roach or a skimmer bream, so I do it fairly often. Allowing the bait to run down with the flow also works on this river, and at intervals when I am doing that I will repeat that 1ft. lift and drop. It is a more efficient approach than lifting out the complete tackle and laying it out in line for another slow drop through the full depth, though that obviously has to be done when the tackle has reached its downstream limit. On moving water of course, you lay the line out in the downstream direction on the re-cast. Working the bait in the manner described, or giving it smaller lifts and drops, is well worth trying on any water.

Another fishery with "regional peculiarities" is the Warwickshire Avon, a river I spend a fair bit of time on. Dace are a key species for the match angler here, and they are usually caught, yet again, on that slow falling bait (Fig 18). The usual system for fishing rivers is to fish that way and then, when the bait reaches bottom, to allow the tackle to go downstream with the flow. On the Avon, however, I find that the dace usually take on the drop all the time, with nothing coming once the bait is on the bottom and being run through. When that is happening I just lift the tackle out when it has dropped all the way, lay it out and let it drop again. That way you are getting the best use of your time. If the bites are all on the drop you fish all the time on the drop, getting the maximum

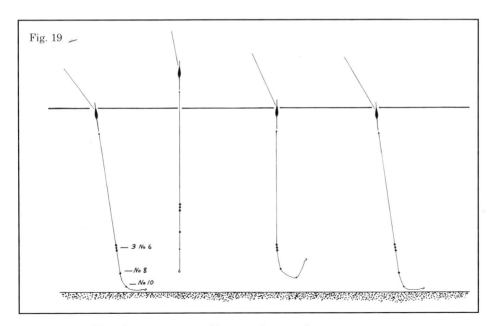

Fig. 19

— 3 No 6
—No 8
— No 10

FLOAT: GROUP C, .40g. or .75g if water is running.
The 1ft. lift and drop method which can provoke bites on rivers like the Witham.

possible number of casts in. It can be, and usually is, the difference between winning and losing. Very often on this river and a good many others winning margins are mere ounces.

This working of the bait is not always possible with rod and reel fishing, simply because we are usually fishing beyond the rod tip. Try lifting a float when you are fishing like that and you will succeed only in dragging the float off line. The pole gives us an extra option, though we must not forget, either, to duplicate the ploys that we can use with the rod and reel. We can check the progress of a float in water which is running even with just a bit of pace. That causes the bait to lift (Fig 20), which frequently attracts bites, particularly at the end of the swim. Repeatedly checking the float on rod and reel, in some conditions, takes the float off line, eventually, but with the pole it is easy to hold back and let go. Try it wherever there is reasonable flow. I am talking about rivers I know well, but it is a move which works on any river.

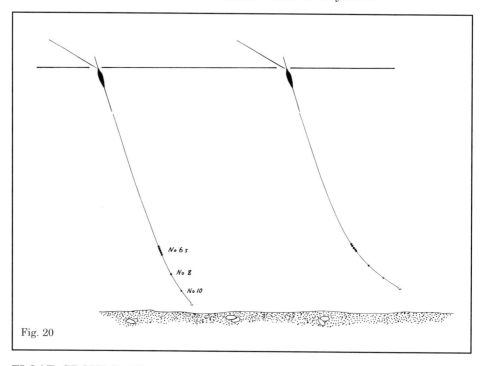

Fig. 20

FLOAT: GROUP B, .75g.
Holding back and releasing river floats, causing the bait to lift and fall, often triggers a bite.

With the pole, as with other methods, you don't have to do anything special to catch fish when they are really having a go. You can do anything and still catch them, but when fish are not feeding well, or are wary, or there aren't many there, it's the angler who works hard, thinks logically and varies his bait presentation who ends up with those extra vital ounces.

By now you may have formed the impression that I hardly ever use olivette weights for still and slow moving water, but that isn't quite the case. It is true that an olivette is rarely if ever the right method for species like roach, skimmers and dace, but it can be better than a full shotting system for bigger bream or hybrids, for instance. Bream in particular like to get their noses into groundbait laced with casters and feeder maggots, and they are usually caught by legering or rod and reel float tackle fished at full depth. Where bream are likely to show within pole range, therefore, there is no point whatsoever in dropping a bait slowly to them. You might as well crash it down as quickly as possible, and there is no quicker way than a tungsten olivette.

The common advice with olivettes seems to be to use them well down the line with a single dropper shot about 6 inches from the hook, and there are times when this is about right. It is a good method when the fish are feeding well. In those circumstances you can catch a lot of small fish quickly, and there is no doubt about the bites. The float will dive under or lift a long way, whereas with light shotting systems the bites can show as very slight indications. Having said all that I am happier with a more sensitive system most of the time. I like to have two droppers, one six inches from the hook, another six inches above it and then the olivette, a further six inches away. That gives me a slower fall of the bait in the last foot, which is handy for those occasions when smaller fish are feeding a bit shyly on or close to bottom (see Fig 21).

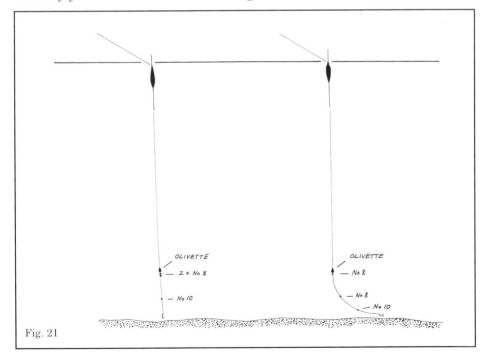

Fig. 21

FLOATS: GROUP C (left) or B (right). Weights can vary from .50g to 2g depending on depth and conditions. *Stopping an olivette with two small shots (left), enables the tackle to be strung out a bit if you want to lay on.*

To have the two dropper option available is simple enough. You may remember previous advice to stop the olivette with two shots placed together, and now is the time to enlarge on that. I was simply preparing the way for variation of the system. When you make the tackle you place one dropper shot near the hook, and then stop the olivette in place on the line using two number 8 shots together, instead of using, say, one number 6 for that job. All you have to do then, to get a two-dropper rig, is to shove the upper number 8 and the olivette six inches up the line.

I certainly like two droppers for the bigger bream. I will usually fish the full depth and then deepen the float by about six inches, to get the lower shot close to bottom or even on it. When bream are feeding they take no catching if you can get the bait in front of them. When legering or waggler float fishing for bream it pays to twitch the bait around the swim quite often, either to provoke a bite or, hopefully, to move the bait from an empty area to where a fish might be feeding. Bream spread out a good bit, like grazing sheep, so rather than leave a bait too long in one place you are more likely to put it in sight of a bream if you do move it. Once again a pole offers a more efficient way of doing this job. With leger, or rod and reel, all you can do is move a bait in a straight line towards you, until eventually it is out of the baited area and a re-cast is necessary. With the pole you can move the bait gradually from one side of the swim to the other and anywhere else in the baited area (Fig 22). You can have an extra section of pole behind where you are actually holding it, which allows you to work a

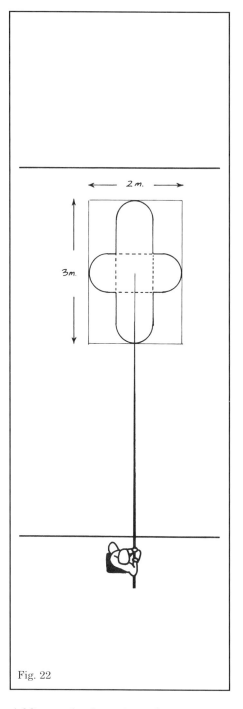

Fig. 22

Adding and subtracting pole sections, and working from side to side, helps you to cover a considerable area of the swim.

bait further out for a metre. By feeding out more pole, moving it around and feeding the pole back behind you it is possible to cover the whole of the baited area in search of bites.

If you are catching bream with some regularity, though, it pays to take them off the edge of the shoal. That way you don't disturb the fish as much as you would by taking them from the middle of the shoal. It can pay, with bream and, indeed, with other species like roach, to work out which way a fish will try to run when you first hook it. Usually it's the opposite direction to the pull, so it can be better to hook them on the far side of the shoal, easing them up and over their companions when they have run out of steam.

Another sound argument for an olivette instead of a light shotting pattern is when fishing stillwaters with a lot of undertow or a river with more than just a steady flow. If you want to hold a bait steady in an undertow, or hold back in a flow, you can do it better with an olivette. You have some weight to hold back against.

FASTER RIVERS

Whilst we can get away with the use of stillwater floats for some jobs on slow rivers there is no chance in faster flows. This is definitely a job for the Group A floats discussed in the chapter covering the correct choice of floats. It should be easy to imagine what happens when a slim-bodied float is held back in fast flow. It will simply lift straight out of the water (Fig 23), and any bite which

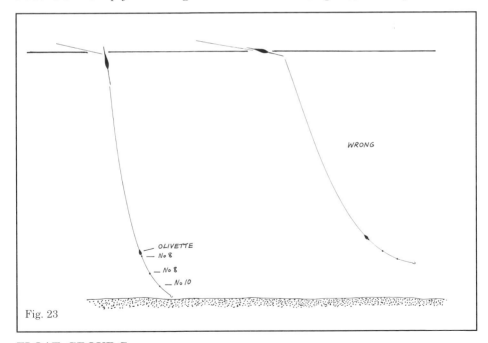

Fig. 23

FLOAT: GROUP C.

Two light a float or the wrong shape of float, on running water can seem right while running through, but when you try to hold back it will lift and lie flat.

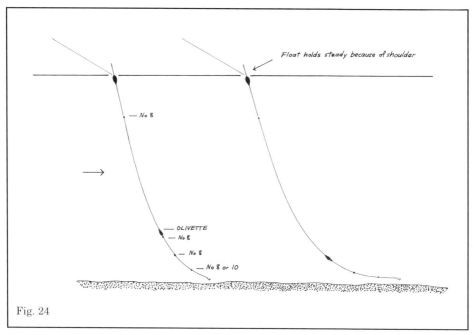

Float holds steady because of shoulder

— No 8

— OLIVETTE
— No 8
— No 8
— No 8 or 10

Fig. 24

FLOAT: GROUP A, .75g.+

Get the float type and size right and you can hold back without the float lifting. If you want to hold back all the time go 1ft. over depth to get the olivette nearer the bottom, as shown on the right.

might come along at that moment would register directly on the pole tip. Providing the right size of Group A round-bodied float is used we do not have that problem. There is enough surface area with a round float for the water to press down on, leaving only the bristle above the surface when you do check the progress of the float (Fig 24).

Finding out which of your round-bodied floats is right for the flow is a trial and error job. If the float is too small for the flow it will still lift when checked, and you need a bigger one. Keep stepping up the size until you get it right, though you may encounter a situation in which none of them will seem to be right. There are times when the pace of the water may cause these floats to lift a bit, even when they are carrying the right amount of weight. The answer is the same as it is when we encounter this problem with rod and reel float fishing methods - we add extra shot to compensate for the lift. It works, but it requires much more effort by the angler. An over-shotted float has to be controlled all the time. If it is allowed to run at the speed of the current it will simply dive under.

We are talking, in the main, of floats taking 1 to 2 grammes of weight, and they will have steel stems to assist stability. More often than not I will be using olivettes for this sort of fishing, simply because you want plenty of weight in one place down the line to hold back against. It is no use having weight spread out all over the place. Stability in this situation depends on float and weight working together to counteract the flow. The tackle will be set about six inches over depth, with the olivette about 2ft from the hook and two dropper shots below it, as in Fig 21. We are nearly always catching on or close to bottom with this method, but I still like the two droppers to give a more natural fall of the bait in that last 2ft. Many are sold on having the olivette lower down, with just one dropper shot, but I don't agree with them. I think I get more bites, most of the time, by doing it my way, but I can always lower my olivette if I want a more tightly controlled bait. It sometimes does attract more bites, usually when the flow is very heavy. It holds the bait down better in that situation, but restricted to one approach it would definitely be the two-dropper system.

Up to now I have described methods of fishing with 2ft to 3ft of line, at most, between pole tip and float. In still and slow water the feeding draws the fish into the effective operating area of a pole with a short line. We can reach as far as we want in those situations, simply by moving the pole and by using a bit more length, but in faster water we need those options plus a longer length of line. We need to be able to reach half way down the peg, and for that we require about six feet of line to the float, sometimes more. It depends on the depth and the speed, but you must be able to drop the float in front of you and work it, under perfect control, to at least half way along the swim, or just past half way. I have stressed the need previously for a short line for the purpose of good control, but here the flow keeps the line dead straight. It helps us to achieve good control with a longer length of line.

It is surprising how far a float can travel in a straight line down the peg with, say, a 10-metre pole (Fig 25). As the float is dropped in directly to the front the

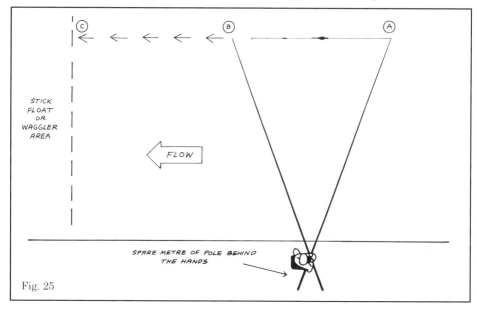

Fig. 25

Covering a river swim with the pole. Lay the tackle in line downstream with the pole at point A. Allowing the float to travel to point B, and following it with the pole, should cover half the swim. Feeding forward with a spare metre of pole kept behind the hands will cover a bit more (not drawn to scale).

pole itself will be angled upstream. As the float travels downstream you simply follow it with the pole, at a speed you can decide. By the time that long pole is angling downstream from where you are sitting, or more likely standing for this method, the float will be half way down the swim. By having a spare section protruding behind where you are holding the pole (providing there is room) you can extend the float's travel by feeding more pole through your hands.

You don't try to fish 10 metres of pole to hand - not unless you are an accomplished pole handler, anyway. The Nottingham angler, Jan Porter, has worked wonders on the Trent with 11 metres to hand, but most anglers could not manage that properly. On that river, or similar rivers, I usually fish five or six metres to hand and unship to land my fish at those lengths. It's nice and comfortable, and I don't see much point in struggling with longer lengths. If it's 10ft deep and you have six feet of line to the float that's five metres, an ideal length to work with for landing your fish. If it's a couple of feet deeper I fish six metres to hand, and ship and unship any extra length I am using. To get the length dead right to swing to hand I adjust the length of line to the float. With six metres in 12ft of water I would probably have 7ft of line to the float. You can't work to one length all the time. You take six feet as an average, but adjust it to suit whatever length of pole you need to work with.

The deeper the water the more comfortable it is, but the depth plus six feet dictates the length of pole you can use to hand. Using that formula a five foot deep swim would give you $11^1/_2$ft of line overall (allowing for fishing six inches over depth). The nearest pole length to that is four metres, so you would need to adjust overall line length to about 12ft.

The overall aim is to use as much of your swim as you can without losing control of the float. If you are loose feeding, as I do for every species except bream and gudgeon, the key area is half way down the peg, as a rule, but fishing the whole way down to that area is always worthwhile. With the olivette rig, in a match, you tend to pick up fish where you can't loose feed. You are nicely placed, though, to catch off the tail end of the loose feed introduced by the angler upstream. If it is very fast, and you can't get loose feed down within the limits of your own swim, it may be too fast for the pole method anyway, though one obvious trick to try is using a bait dropper on a spare pole, introducing feed at the top end of the peg. Some time ago we adapted the standard bait dropper, fixing a longer release mechanism - 2 to 3ft long brass rod with a heavy weight on the end - to open the dropper well off the bottom. Since then we have seen a new type of dropper which can be lowered to the required depth and opened with a sharp lift of the spare pole.

One way or another there's always a method of getting loose feed into the right place, though I rarely pole fish fast water without the back-up of stick float or waggler tackle. When the time comes that I can get bites only at the extreme limit of pole range I switch to the stick, and it is always a good idea in the last hour of a match to fish the last half to one third of the swim with rod and reel. There will be fish there which are feeding with total confidence, because they have not been disturbed.

If your waters respond to groundbait you are laughing with the pole. There are areas of the Trent which produce plenty of skimmers to groundbait and caster, and the aim is to get the groundbait, mixed fairly solid, onto the bottom as near to the front as you can get it. I don't mean to mix the bait like concrete. It has to break up slowly to release the casters. One useful fast water tip, which came from Bob Nudd, I believe, is to lace the groundbait with pea gravel to make it literally sink like a stone. Once on the bottom the gravel simply becomes a harmless part of the river bed.

Tactically speaking there isn't much to fast water fishing. The fish are usually in the bottom 2ft, so there isn't much shot shuffling to do, other than trying minor changes in the distance of the bottom shot to the hook. It's rare for the fish to come well off bottom, but it can happen in warmer conditions in summer. If it does the olivette rig should come off in favour of an even string of size 4 or 6 shots, fished stick float style. Before trying that, though, I might move the olivette gradually higher up the line, to see if that will cope with the situation.

Speed of bait presentation varies a bit. To begin with I usually run the float through steadily, not much slower than the speed of the current, and continue with that while I am getting bites. When the bites dry up I slow the tackle up, holding back much more. Then I will try stopping the float at intervals, hoping that the consequent rise and fall of the bait will provoke some action. Quite often the float will go down as soon as you let it go after checking. It is similar to what we do while stick float fishing, but it is so much easier with the pole. As you hold the float the bait rides up in the water, and it seems to drop the bait into a fish's mouth as soon as you release the float.

A reminder on elastics. It has to be no. 5 or blue code elastic for this fishing, for there is no telling what you might hook. A big fish on lighter elastic is virtually out of control in fast water. It takes too much out, and you have a real job on your hands to land it.

WHEN TO USE WAGGLERS

Delightful though it is to fish with the Continental-style pole floats with the rings on the bodies, and the sensitive bristles, it is not always possible to use them. Indeed there are situations in which waggler type floats, which are attached bottom end only, are much more effective. One obvious situation is on a stillwater where the wind is very strong. I have already mentioned how we change to a different type of stillwater float with a more elongated body to beat the wind, but it can be too strong for that to work. The answer is a waggler float, and while there are a number of alternatives I think the smaller of the crystal floats, which have fine tip inserts, are superior to most. One use for them is covered in the bleak fishing chapter, but in a bad blow on a lake or canal they are used for a different purpose.

The wind will straighten the usual 2ft of line between the pole tip and float, and will also cause the pole tip to vibrate. On a tight line the pole float, attached Continental style, will jerk around in response to every movement of the pole tip. Fishing a waggler instead can solve that problem, for you can dip the pole tip just under the surface and sink the line (Fig 26). With the line under water

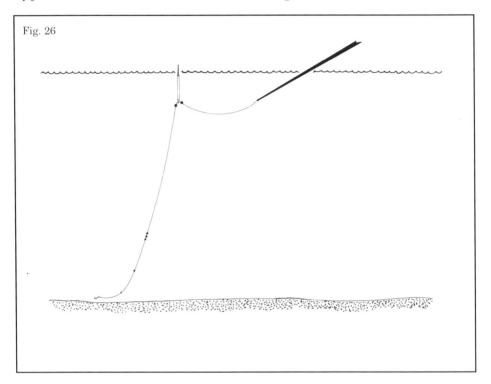

Fig. 26

FLOAT: GROUP E, 3BB.

If the wind is awkward push the pole tip under the surface to sink the line.

you can then move the pole tip right next to the float, and no matter how much the wind moves the pole it won't move the float. The line between them is too slack for that to happen. Sometimes that's enough, but there could be times when the wind sets the water moving, and the float will not hold position with a slack line.

The best alternative, to maintain control and still avoid float movement, is to back shot the waggler, putting a no. 8 shot on the line between the float and the pole (Fig 27). It can help to have a slightly longer line, say 3ft instead of 2ft, but if you are stuck with the shorter length it still works. The effect of the shot is to create an angle in the line below the surface, and you are also creating a sort of shock absorber for the float. As the wind blows the pole towards the float the effect is absorbed by the shot sinking a bit, and as the pole wags back the other way the shot lifts up again. The float itself stays still. A further plus is that the angle in the line reduces the chance of a quick bite rattling on the pole tip,

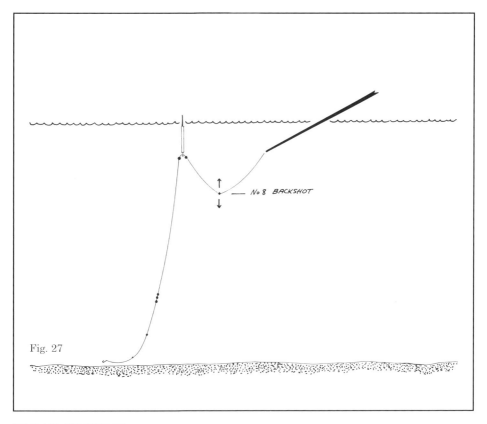

Fig. 27

No 8 BACKSHOT

FLOAT: GROUP E.

When the wind is bouncing the pole tip, and therefore moving the float, the way out is to create an angle between the two, using a back shot. Pole movement is then absorbed by the shot moving about – not the float.

which usually makes the fish let go. Obviously the no.8 used as a back shot has to be taken from the line below the float. It cannot be an additional shot because its weight still registers on the float.

Another case for the small waggler is when fishing a shallow canal with a long pole and the usual short line. You might be fishing the far shelf at 11 metres, in only 18 inches of water, which means you are using less than 4ft of line altogether. You have to drop the float in at the nearside, put the pole together and push the float right across. Then you lift it off and lay the tackle out, usually shotted to fall through nice and slow. The trouble is that with a small float attached via a ring and on the stem you will get a lot of tangles during that process, but with a little waggler that almost never happens. You also have the same back-shotting option just described, if the wind is a problem.

Wagglers are often essential, too, for situations in which you might want to fish beyond the length of your pole (Fig 28 overleaf). This applies to lakes or canals, but let us stay with the example of the canal. You might have an 11 metre pole and the far shelf is actually a further metre away. To reach it you

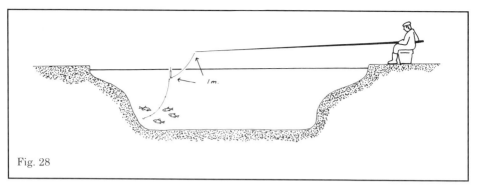

Fig. 28

FLOAT: GROUP E.

Fishing beyond the pole tip on the far shelf of a canal.

can have a metre of line to the pole float and, when the tackle has been taken across, you just lift up the pole and cast the extra distance. It is done with a movement which almost exactly matches how you would do it with rod and reel float tackle at close range. You lift the pole, then lower it and push forward simultaneously. That lays out the tackle perfectly in a direct line away from you. It is perhaps best for beginners and the less experienced to practice this move at closer range with a much shorter pole. That way you will soon realise what is required with the longer set-up. Obviously it helps to have a following wind or no wind at all, but if there is a breeze the back-shot set-up will again be useful. If you can get away with simply sinking the line instead that is preferable to the back-shot.

Before the advent of such long poles we would have had to tackle that kind of situation with a waggler float carrying much more shot overall, simply because it has to be cast the distance. You wouldn't get a float carrying a few small shots that far, and the further handicap is the length of line the rod and reel method requires us to have under the surface. With small fish in particular the weight of the float and the resistance of the sunken line combine to cause us to miss far too many bites. For some reason, too, it is possible to get no bites at all on waggler tackle - nothing that can be seen on the float, anyway - while the light pole approach will catch fish. To give one example, I can remember fishing the Market Weighton Canal with a waggler and with leger tackle, on a day when a strong wind was blowing. It had been too strong for me to consider putting a pole up, but when neither the waggler nor the leger produced any bites I rigged a pole late in the match.

For some reason the switch to a 12-metre pole and small waggler produced a bite every cast for the rest of the match. I had put a longer than normal length of line on, one metre instead of 2ft, and by casting beyond the end of the pole I was getting the float in about the same place as I had been casting with rod and reel. The wind was bouncing the pole and the float was dragging about a bit, but the bites were coming. I can only think it was a combination of two factors - the bait movement, plus the difference in the relative weights of the two tackles. I had been using a $2^1/_2$ AAA waggler, but with the pole I was able to use a waggler taking just 2BB. If it hadn't been for the wind I could have gone much lighter. I wish I could say it was a piece of clever inspiration, but it was nothing like that. I was talking to a friend about pole fishing, and I thought I might as well try it and give him a demonstration at the same time. I could not believe it when I got an eel the first cast, and then another five, one after the other.

I have previously dealt with the methods of catching on the drop with continental floats, but in some situations it can be done as well or even better with a waggler float. Sometimes in windy conditions you want a bit of weight around the float for ease of casting, but with only a couple of small shots down the line to achieve the necessary slow fall of the bait. Briefly it has virtually all the weight locking the float in place, and two little ones down the line. Using the same amount of weight on a top and bottom float would mean bulking it down the line, and defeating the object - the slow fall of the bait from surface to bottom. That's a crude but effective way of fishing for relatively uneducated fish, but the method is easily miniaturised. I often use it with a small waggler locked on the line with two no. 4s, and with two 8s or an 8 and a 10 down the line (Fig 29).

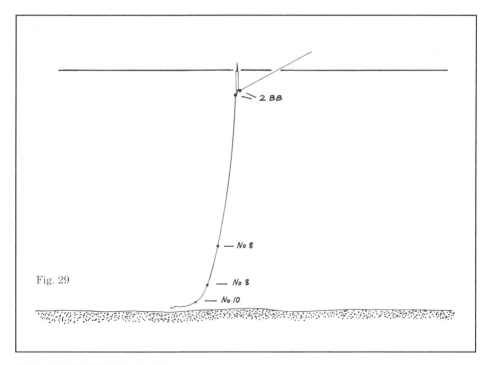

Fig. 29

FLOAT: GROUP E, $2^1/_2$ BB.
Waggler rig for drop fishing.

SCRAPING FOR BLOODWORM & JOKER

by Tom Pickering

There are anglers who complain about the difficulty of obtaining bloodworm, or about the cost of buying this bait. They are usually the same people who campaign for it to be banned in matches. I don't really mind whether or not bloodworm and jokers are banned, for whatever the rules are they are the same for everyone, but I certainly don't go along with the complaints. It is easy to collect these baits, and anyone who buys them at fancy prices is wasting his money. Perhaps they have been put off by the apparently difficult and complicated advice which has been given in the past on how to collect bloodworm - usually from professional scrapers with no vested interest in making it sound easy.

All stillwaters hold bloodworms, and they are a natural food for the fish. Some are better than others, and the best water for bloodworm is one which has a gravel or hard bottom beneath a top layer of silt. I have found that waters with lots of bloodworm are great for producing feed worms for loose-feeding or to put in groundbait. Those with fewer worms seem to produce bigger samples which are perfect for the hook. Give me an hour and I can get enough of both kinds for any match, and a few pints of jokers takes even less time. So much for the difficulties.

I do not profess to be an expert on the subject, nor do I make the claim that my method is the best available. All I know is that it suits me well enough, and I am confident I can always get enough bait if I can find a spare hour the day or evening before a match in which bloodworm is likely to be the key. I am hoping to tell the story best in pictures and captions, but I will just run quickly through the equipment and procedure.

Bloodworm has to be scraped from the bottom silt with an angled metal scraper fitted to a pole. The colder the water the deeper the worms congregate, which tends to be a disadvantage, but they are generally in a depth we can reach with chest waders. I take a big maggot bowl with me, tied to my waders so it won't drift away. The bowl in half full of water, and submerged in it is a small maggot-sized riddle. I scrape the bottom, and knock whatever comes up on the scraper - usually mud, debris and bloodworm - onto the side of the bowl. It falls into the riddle, and the bloodworms separate themselves by wriggling through the mesh into the water below.

Close-up of the angled tool used to scrape bloodworms from the bottom silt of ponds and lakes. Note the bloodworms draped over the leading edge.

After each scrape the results are tapped into a floating container. This is part-filled with water, and should be tied to the angler. Ideally it should float down wind, just far enough away to be within comfortable reach of the scraper.

Inside the box is a fine mesh riddle which collects any leaves, weed or rubbish. The bloodworms wriggle through it into the water below.

Water and bloodworms are then poured into a much finer meshed riddle – some anglers use flour riddles or ladies' stockings.

78

Any remaining silt is then rinsed off leaving the angler with neat bloodworms.

After rinsing the bloodworms are kept in loose, flat paper parcels, ready for use.

Sometimes I have to scrape around for a while before I find a dense concentration of bloodworm, but it takes only a few minutes in a productive area to get several pints. To give you an idea of the possibilities I once scraped for 40 minutes and got 13 pints! Nowadays I'm a better judge of what I am getting, so when I think I have enough for a match I wade to the bank, and throw away the rubbish which has collected in the riddle. Then I tip the contents of the bowl into a fine mesh riddle or an ordinary flour sieve and wash it in the lake. In a few seconds I have clean, solid worm. I know there are better ways than that, but it's OK for me. It is simple, effective and it gets me what I want in a short time. I tip the washed worms onto three sheets of newspaper in quantities of about threequarters of a pint per package. Any more than that seems too much to keep well. I spread the worms out, and wrap each lot up into a neat, flat parcel. The bait will keep perfectly well until I get it home. All I do then is change the paper, because the original will have got too soggy. It should keep well in the second parcel for at least 24 hours, though it can pay to have a look at it earlier than that. If it seems a bit dry, spray a little water on the bait. You will be fishing with perfectly fresh bait, and to be properly effective bloodworm has to be fresh. I don't keep it beyond the second day after it has been collected, though it is possible to keep it longer in a cool place. Rather than that, though, I would go and collect some more.

If I was after a lot of bait I might need a different system, but I am not writing this for the benefit of would-be commercial collectors, who end up over-scraping waters and have to go further and further afield for the bait. I'm just passing

Jokers are collected in exactly the same way, but from shallow streams and using a shorter handled scraper.

on a good method for individual anglers. If you can find a good water, and scrape it for yourself, you will have an endless supply whenever you need it. Scraping jokers is just as easy, probably easier. I won't bore my readers with the entomology by going into the difference between the two types of insect larvae. All you need to know is that jokers are like miniature bloodworms - too small for the hook but good as a feeder when bloodworm is used as the bait - and that they are found in streams, not lakes. Streams which are polluted, or which receive effluent from a sewage outfall, seem to be the best source, though why I am not sure. Maybe it is because they thrive where there is little or no other natural life to predate on them, but the reason isn't important either.

It did not take me long to find a stream with a sewage outfall in South Yorkshire! I am tempted to suggest you ask your local fisheries department where their pollution watchdogs down the corridor are not doing their job properly, but the approach might not be appreciated. Once you have found a source, though, the rest is simple. I use more or less the same method described for bloodworm. I have a short-handled scraper, because the water I use is only a foot deep, the same bowl and a pinkie riddle inside it. It has a smaller mesh than a maggot riddle. Then I just walk upstream, scraping as I go, and if I don't have two solid pints of joker in 20 minutes it will be more than a little surprising. The place is red raw with joker. I could get six pints in an hour, but two pints is enough for a day's fishing. Some anglers do it a different way, scraping with fine mesh nets. Take your pick. Once again I am only describing a method which suits me.

About 12 pints of jokers, the product of two men's efforts in two hours.

FISHING WITH BLOODWORM

by Tom Pickering

There are different ways of fishing bloodworm on different venues, and I will try to deal with them all. The continental method of banging in hopefully the entire feed supply for a match, right at the start, has applications over here, and perhaps I should deal with that first. The aim is to introduce solid balls of bait which carry large amounts of bloodworm and joker - enough to attract and hold a shoal of fish without adding any more, certainly not in big balls, at any rate. We have to get the bloodworm and joker distributed right through the groundbait, and it isn't as straightforward as it sounds. The bait bunches up, and the best way to break it apart is to add a bit of dry leam, which is available from good tackle shops. Leam separates the bloodworms very well, leaving no big lumps, and when it is mixed into the groundbait it is evenly distributed. There is another type of leam – wet leam – which is used as a constituent of the groundbait. A typical mix would be one third wet leam, one third standard

An important stage in preparation of groundbait for bloodworm fishing. Dry leam is mixed with jokers and / or bloodworms to separate them. Without it they knot up into bunches.

The bloodworm feed and leam are added to the chosen groundbait mix...

...and the leam ensures a nice, even distribution of the bloodworms and jokers.

Bloodworm / joker "bombs" ready mixed for the initial bombardment method.

breadcrumb groundbait, and one third Continental groundbait, Sensas, Van den Eynde, or whatever is your choice. These are aromatic baits designed to attract fish, and I have more to say about them elsewhere.

The important thing about the mix is that it should be smooth and firm when it is ready to go in, and not sticky. I have tried and failed to come up with a form of words which would put more meaning into that. Whatever quantity of bait I mix I manage to get it right, either by instinct or experience, and you will learn more by mixing a few batches yourself than you will from reading about it. The main essential is to get a non-sticky mix which will be firm enough to throw and hit bottom without breaking up. Once on the bottom it should break down reasonably quickly, releasing bloodworms and/or jokers to be mopped up by the fish. You are aiming, in effect, to create an artificial bottom to your swim - a carpet loaded with goodies; a place where the fish will want to stay for quite some time.

Five minutes before the start of a match I will make the balls up ready for throwing, and the quantity depends on the water, and what you know it will take. I can't give you a formula for every water, but a bombardment for this method could be anything from six big balls to as many as 20. I will tell you how to work out more accurately what is required in a while. Most of the time, however, I go in with about 10, and leave it at that, but on still or very slow water

Our "heavy baiting" methods are kid's stuff in comparison to the continental approach. This World Championship competitor has thirty "grapefruits" ready to throw and he still has another mix at his feet!

one of them will be different to the other nine. The very first ball I throw will be mixed wetter and softer than the rest. It is made to explode on impact, showering out the contents and colouring up the water. That's my attractor, to bring fish in. The other balls will crash through the cloud, and I'm ready for what is hopefully going to be several hours of good sport. On faster water the soft ball tactic doesn't work, because the cloud effect will go off downstream.

When British anglers first saw this heavy baiting approach they were absolutely stunned. It seemed certain to scare fish to the horizon, but the Continentals knew what they were doing. In fact it has the opposite effect, drawing fish in and holding them. It is amazing how often you can do this, introducing many thousands of feed worms, and get a bite the instant you drop in with the bait. But maybe I have got a bit ahead of myself. One obvious

Holding the chosen length of pole in one hand, and throwing groundbait with the other, gives you an exact marker to aim at.

requirement is accuracy in the throwing. You have to get the bait to the end of whatever length of pole you have decided to use. Some anglers will set their pole in the rests fixed to their baskets, or wherever, and aim their feed at the tip of the pole. Others, me included, hold the pole in one hand, and throw with the other. That way you are sure of getting it in the right place. With the other way you have to make allowance for the fact that the pole is longer in the hands than it is in the rests. You either have to have an extra section on, and work it out from there, or throw the feed a bit further if the intended length of pole is in the rests. Sounds complicated, but it isn't, really. Which method is best for you depends on how accurate a thrower you are. Probably the pole in the rests is better if you aren't an instinctively good thrower.

Clearly this method is intended to produce bites on or near the bottom, so it

The alternative if you aren't good enough with the "wrong" hand. The pole can be held in rests on the box while you throw with your better hand.

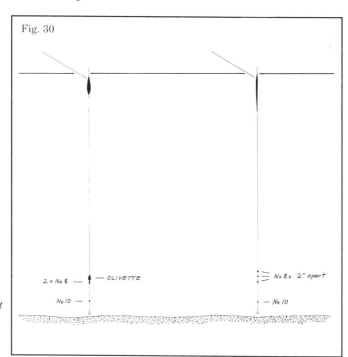

Fig. 30

**FLOATS:
GROUP C or D
.25g to 1.5g
(depending on
depth).**

*Standard olivette rig
for bloodworm fishing
(left) and the light shot
alternative.*

calls for the use of olivettes, fished with just one dropper shot, as in the left hand side of Fig 30. (The right hand drawing is of an alternative, light shotting rig for bloodworm fishing in shallow water). On moving water we require a round patterned float; on stillwaters one of the more elongated floats, depending on the wind conditions up top. Exactly where to employ the bombardment approach is a more difficult question, but basically it's for waters which hold a lot of fish. Other methods of feeding bloodworm, which I will come to shortly, create far too much activity off the bottom on waters with large fish populations. Despite all I have said about catching on the drop you don't want to create that situation with bloodworm, with a lot of fish around. It sends them crazy, dashing about at all levels, and the float gets knocked around so much you can't read or hit the bites properly. It's far better with an olivette and one dropper, which attract nice, positive bites.

If you get the initial feeding right there won't be any need to feed again, though we aren't always that smart. You have to fish a water a few times to get the feel of it. One thing you have to find out the hard way - so find out when you are practising - is whether the water will take another bait bombardment if and when the bites eventually start to tail off. Some will, others won't. On a water which won't respond to further heavy baiting it pays to put more in at the start. Try 15 instead of 10. If it will take more there's no problem, but the situation isn't utterly hopeless if the swim is dying too soon and you know it won't take even one more big ball. You can quietly introduce more neat bloodworm or joker via the little cup accessories, which clip to the ends of poles. You carefully

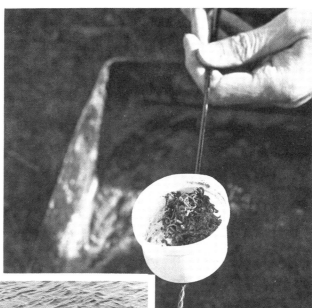

For "top-up" feeding neat bloodworms can be put into a cup, which is clipped on the end section of the pole near the tip.

The cup is then carefully extended to the right position, and upended to feed the swim with pinpoint accuracy.

extend the pole to the right position and turn the cup upside down, but it is not a tactic I use all that often.

I always ask myself why a swim is dying. Are there fish there which need more feed, or have they gone? If I think they have gone I will try to attract some more in by feeding some small but soft balls, creating something like the cloud effect mentioned earlier. If I think they are still there, but need more feed, I will put in a tangerine-sized ball of harder bait in - but only if I know they will take it. This is an alternative to a further heavy bombardment, which I don't really like to risk. If I know a water won't take any further hard balls of bait I will resort to introducing neat bloodworm and joker via the cup. Whenever you are faced with the need to add more bait, however, make a mental note to increase the initial feeding next time. It may need 20 balls, but by trial and error you will eventually come up with an approach which is about right most of the time.

I emphasised the importance of plumbing the depth earlier, and it is never more important than it is when bloodworm fishing. Before I decide on the length of pole to use I will plumb around to find any bumps or depressions. If I find a little ledge at, say 8 metres, I will concentrate my feed on that, rather than fish a flatter area at 10 or 11 metres. I have noticed some anglers will always use whatever length of pole they are most comfortable with, and so will I if there aren't any features to concentrate on. If there is one there, though, I will use it. I will plumb the exact depth at that point and shorten off by exactly half an inch. What happens from this point is common to most other ways of fishing bloodworm, so I will go into it right away.

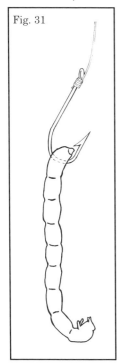

Fig. 31

The bloodworm is hooked through the head (Fig 31). Then you drop the float in the water, ship the pole and lower the tackle straight down onto the baited area. It will be a bit of a surprise if the float doesn't go first cast, and on the good days it will keep on going down, or lifting up on the bristle, for quite a while. While that is happening you have nothing special to do, except lift the pole gently to hook your fish, unship the pole to swing fish in or net them, and mechanically repeat the whole process. There is no need to work the bait or manipulate the float in any way. Just concentrate on a nice steady rhythm, and catch all the easy fish you can. Unless you are very lucky, though, it won't last for ever.

The bloodworm is hooked through the head.

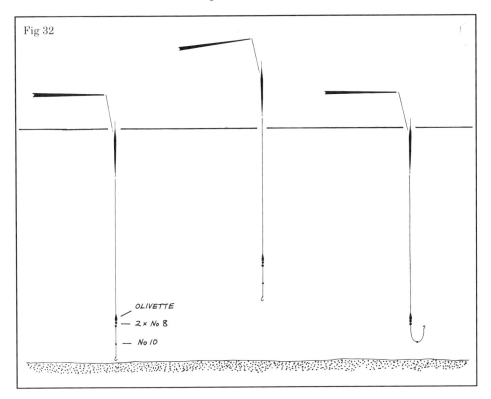

Fig 32

OLIVETTE

— 2 × No 8

— No 10

FLOAT: GROUP D.

A 6" lift and drop of the tackle imitates the "jump" which bloodworms sometimes perform naturally. It often provokes a bite.

There will come a time when the shoal has been thinned out, and the remainder are more wary. The bites will slow down, or even stop altogether, and it's from here on that you have to start working for your fish. One tactic which never seems to fail is to lift the float six inches out of the water and drop it straight back in (Fig 32). Very often the float will just carry on going as a fish takes the bait. If you have ever watched bloodworms in a bucket or a glass container you will have some idea why this movement can trigger bites. Every now and again a bloodworm will jump up from the bottom for about six inches, and sink back down again. It must happen in their natural habitat, and fish must be used to seeing it and taking advantage of it.

Another tactic is a less emphatic movement of the float. With the line running from the eye, set down the body of the float, a steady pull on the pole will cause the float to lift. You are doing it right if the float lifts about half an inch, obviously causing the bait to lift a little too (Fig 33 overleaf). That also provokes bites when the fish are getting shy. For some reason the six inch lift encourages bites mostly from the smaller fish. The smaller movement generally seems to bring rather bigger fish, sometimes much bigger, though I have yet to understand why. It is dangerous to credit fish with human failings, but it is almost as though the fish has been eyeing a meal without really wanting it until it looks like getting away, perhaps to be snapped up by another fish. We know this form of behaviour is common to many fish, including predators like pike. Any pike man will tell you he has had a deadbait out for hours, only to get a take seconds after the bait has been tweaked along the bottom a short way. Movement clearly triggers either an aggressive reaction or a feeding response, and match anglers have to take advantage of that knowledge.

It is a common experience when bloodworm fishing to catch mostly the smaller fish first, which is why my first tactic, when activity starts to slow down, is the six inch lift. I will keep doing that while it is working well, but when it stops working the swim can seem quite dead. One of two things has happened, then. You have either overdone the feeding, and the fish have finally filled up, or bigger fish have moved in and shoved the smaller ones out. The shorter tweak on the float produces, in the main, a better sample of fish when there is a mix of sizes in the swim. When a swim goes dead because it has been invaded by bigger fish they are often a good bit bigger than anything which was there originally. Fine, you may say. Just go on giving the float those little tweaks, but I don't think that's the best way to get some of

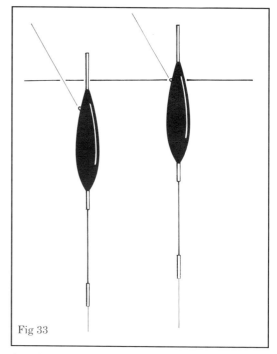

Fig 33

Another bite-inducing bloodworm tactic. A slight and steady pull causes a half inch lift of the float and a corresponding lift of the bait as shown in 33A. The bait is then allowed to fall back quickly to the bottom.

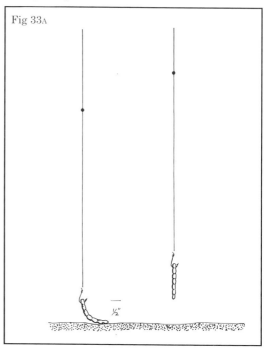

Fig 33A

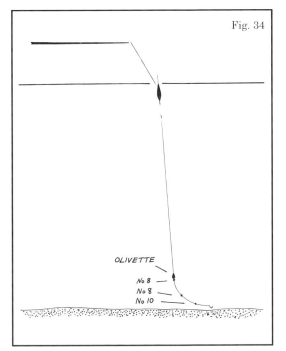

Fig. 34

FLOAT: GROUP C or D, .50g.+ (depending on depth).

An olivette rig "strung out" to present a bunch of bloodworms 6" over depth.

those bonus newcomers.

It's almost gospel for bloodworm anglers to fish the bait that critical half inch off bottom - head up, tail in mud, perfectly natural presentation. But I don't think it is right for big fish. They don't go around delicately selecting individual bloodworms. They get their noses in the bottom silt and go sifting for them. Before carp anglers went boilie crazy a key tactic was to drop a bunch of redworms into silt for bloodworm-sifting carp to find. I don't suggest that we should fish quite like that, but it helps to make the point that bigger fish feed in different ways. When I suspect the presence of big fish on my bloodworm I deepen the float to lay six inches of line on the bottom, and lift the olivette six inches higher, giving me a more sensitive terminal tackle (Fig 34). Then I just sit and hold the tackle steady. Those bigger fish will move around, sucking at the silt, and sooner or later one or two will find the bloodworm with the hook in it. When they have their heads down, and perhaps are clouding up the bottom, they aren't going to find a bait which is above where they are operating.

Another obvious tactic when bigger fish are looking for a mouthful is to give them one. I will put two, three, four or even more worms on the hook. We call it "giving them a blob of jam." It looks good enough to eat yourself. They will find it, but there is nothing to stop you moving the bait around as previously described, if sitting and waiting doesn't produce the goods.

That's the heavy baiting method and the tactical side of bloodworm fishing, but it isn't the only approach. One major alternative is the "drip-feed" method of groundbaiting on the waters which do not respond to the bombardment approach. England international Bob Nudd is particularly good at this method. It's mainly for canals where a few pounds of small fish is likely to win, or other waters where fish populations are not vast and the fish are not particularly big. Little roach, perch, gudgeon and sometimes bleak are the main targets. The groundbait will be the same type as we use for the bombardment approach, and whether it is soft or hard depends on what species we are after. For bleak, roach,

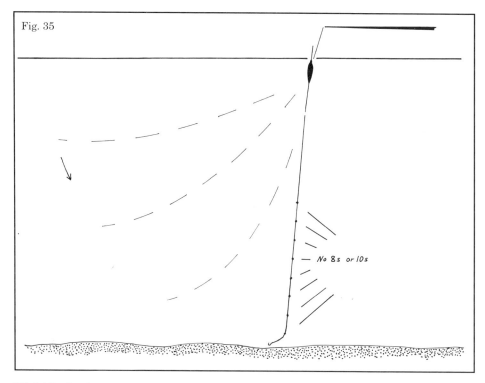

Fig. 35

No 8s or 10s

FLOAT: GROUP B, .50g.

Drop fishing with bloodworm requires light, even shotting over the bottom two thirds of the line.

dace and perch it would be soft, to cloud the water and to allow us to catch on the drop. You just mix it up with more water in, introducing a little ball of slop every cast. You have the terminal tackle falling through the cloud all the time with tackle which is similar but not the same as described for drop fishing with maggot on stillwaters. You go through the same routine with a different bait, in effect.

The difference in the shotting is small but important. Instead of even shotting, stick float style, we have the shot distributed over the bottom two thirds of the line (Fig 35). The aim is to have smaller shots closer together so that the tackle falls like a pendulum - a pendulum going one way, anyway! It's a bit more rigid, in effect, and it shows a bite on the float the instant a fish takes the bait. It simply stops the float settling, and it is immediately recognisable as a bite. It's busy fishing - laying out the tackle, watching it sink to the full depth, out and in again, and those little balls of bait go in every single cast.

For gudgeon we use the groundbait harder, mixing it with less water, and aim to have it breaking up immediately after hitting bottom. Because you want to get down quickly then the shotting is different. It has to be more bunched, as in Fig 36,or perhaps a small olivette and dropper. With both methods we are usually fishing quite close, and swinging the fish to hand. We have the short

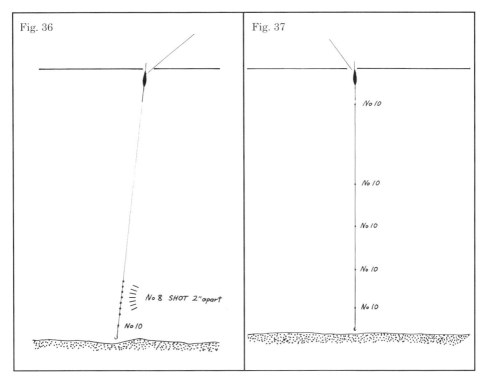

Fig. 36

Fig. 37

No 10

No 10

No 10

No 10

No 10

No 8 SHOT 2" apart

No 10

FLOAT: GROUP C (stillwater) or B (moving), .40g.

Gudgeon rig for bloodworm. Stringing out the No. 8s two inches apart achieves a more attractive fall of the bait in the last few inches.

FLOAT: GROUP C, .10g.

The light tackle used by the Barnsley team for an important match on the Bolton Canal. It is designed to catch very small fish at all levels.

length of line to the float for good control and positive striking. Beyond 3 or 4 metres we keep the short line to the float using extra sections, and shipping and unshipping as required, but the method is most effective if we can fish to hand.

The bombardment and drip-feeding are the main methods with the bloodworm, but they are not the whole story. There are venues where we might be looking to catch just a pound of fish, as a target weight in a team event. One example which springs to mind is the Bolton Canal, where my Barnsley team had to qualify for the DFDS Seaways final. On this water 1 to 2lbs is a good weight, and you might be catching 30 to 40 fish in five hours. We approached this with very light tackle (Fig 37) - three to four number 10 shot strung out evenly to begin with - and with a small amount of groundbait at the start. The float was a small cane-stemmed job which slowly cocked as the little shots registered, and we went through the entire drop fishing routine described in the Techniques and Tactics chapter. It was the same job in miniature - slow fall with shots strung out, reading the float and adjusting where necessary, bunching shot, going a bit over depth, stringing the shot out again, coming a bit off bottom, the lot. It was a constant battle for the odd bite, but on that water we would not have got any with tackle a bit heavier. The feeding, we felt, had to be with bloodworm and joker as neat as possible - neat in the tot of whisky sense, not as in tidy!

There are several ways of achieving that. You can mix a bit of wet leam into solid bloodworm or joker, just enough to clog the bait and hold it together when it is squeezed up and thrown. A sprinkling of Sticky Mag, normally used for binding maggots together for throwing or catapulting, also works well. The cup method previously mentioned is a more practicable proposition with the shorter poles. Some anglers upend it under water while others drop it on the top; I don't think it matters which. The one big plus is that it drops the

For "top-up" feeding neat bloodworms can be mixed with a bit of wet leam, squeezed into a ball and thrown.

feed exactly where you are fishing, every time. I don't use it much because I think it slows me down, and I am happier throwing the bait. I mentioned the use of dry leam to separate bloodworms which tend to get bound together, but in this case the problem turns into an advantage. You can just pick a lump out of the paper and throw it in totally neat. Obviously you can't throw it a long way, but 3 to 4 metres is no problem, and I have thrown it to 8 metres in the right conditions.

There is no need to use groundbait to get bloodworms and jokers to the bottom. Just chuck them in and watch. They dive down to the bottom like lightning, which is one of the reasons for shotting only the bottom two thirds of the tackle for drop fishing. The fish don't get much chance to feed in the top third! More and more anglers are resorting to neat feeding wherever they can manage it, but in the main I prefer groundbait because I feel it attracts fish into the swim.

That's the basis of the game, but having read through it all I realise there is still scope for a few more random bits of information. How do you know, for example, when the fish have just about eaten up the food supply? One key indicator on most if not all waters is that when they have cleaned up all the feed you will suddenly start getting a lot of bites quickly. If that happens do not assume that a big shoal of new and hungry fish has arrived. It's a bad sign. The fish that are left are effectively competing for one worm - the one on the hook! You will get that mad rush of bites, but then they will be away, looking for somebody else's patch of bloodworm. So when that silly period of hectic action begins you have to recognise it and act quickly, feeding again in whatever way you think they will take it - another hard ball, a bit of slop or whatever. You have nothing to lose, really. If they go because you don't feed you might not get them back. If they go because you have fed, therefore, it's no loss.

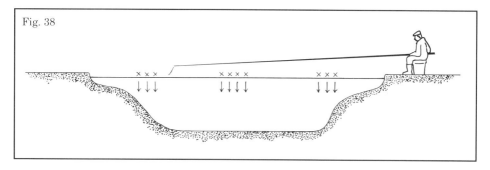

Fig. 38

On a canal always feed the near and far shelves, plus the middle if it is wide enough and there is not much boat traffic.

Exactly where to feed is another subject worth considering (Fig 38). On small canals it's a near shelf and far shelf job, but on a wider canal like, say, the Leeds/Liverpool I will probably put the main initial bombardment in the middle, and put softer bait on the near and far shelves. I fish the near line until the bites run out, leaving the other two swims to settle down, and concentrate mostly on the middle and the far side from then on. I will feed the near side again, after the bites have dried up, just in case I need to come back onto it, but basically I am expecting the majority of the catch from the other two areas.

Hooks for bloodworm fishing? They have to be fine wire, but not the very fine, long-shanked hooks which were developed for continental fishing. I don't like them at all. I use the normal fine wire crystal bend hooks in sizes 20, 22 and 24, mostly. The 22 is the common one. For a bunch of worms it will be a 20, with the 24 when they are on the shy side. When they are going barmy one worm on an 18 will often catch a fish a throw. It's a case of sorting out what's best on the day. You have to get the bites, and land the fish. If you are losing too many step up a size. If you still get the bites that's fine, but if not you have to drop back down again and tolerate the losses. With maggot fishing we don't swap around as much, but with bloodworm it all depends how many fish are there. With a lot of fish dashing around competing they will have a bigger hook.

HIGH SPEED BLEAKING

by Tom Pickering

Quote:

> *"Everything he is said to have done he's done. The 35lb bleak catch in five hours, the 22lbs in three hours, everything. He is one of those annoying blokes who succeed without needing to try... but we haven't seen the best of him yet."*

(England team manager Dick Clegg, talking about Tom Pickering in Coarse Angler magazine in July 1977, when Clegg was then the Barnsley National Championship team skipper - CD).

That quote gave me quite a kick at the time, but it wasn't all that accurate as a prophesy - not if he was suggesting that I would go on to take much bigger bleak weights, anyway. My weights were taken at a time when the River Trent was at a peak for bleak, and not long afterwards it declined. Fewer and fewer swims had big bleak catch potential, and I did not draw any of them. The method, as a possible match winner, has gone into cold storage, until the species makes a comeback, but the basics of it are still vital for weight building, section winning and, of course, for team points events such as winter leagues and the National Championships.

The present situation is not one I particularly grieve about, for I don't actually like bleak fishing. I had to master it as an essential skill, but I have always regretted that I came to the fore with it just a bit too late. A year or so earlier it might have got me into the 1976 England team for the famous bleak match in Bulgaria, though by all accounts the team didn't know what was facing them until they actually got there. It was in that year that I got 24lbs 5oz of bleak in a five hour match on the tidal Trent at Collingham. I'd also done 35lbs in five hours in a timed practice session against Denis White, and in front of plenty of witnesses. In 1977 I did 22lbs in three hours at Shelford, only to get a rollicking from Denis, who reckoned I'd thrown away the chance to set an all-time bleak record in a five hour match by not starting early enough. He wasn't impressed by my excuse that I'd gone for them as soon as they had showed.

At the time I was easily capable of 250 bleak an hour, and when I look at Dino Bassi's return of 364 fish in 90 minutes, in Bulgaria, I always start to dream. Could I have taken him, off level pegs? According to those who were there Bassi never had a slow spell. In all my better catches I'd had periods struggling for bites, taking about 14 fish one minute and only one or two the next. The dream always ends the same way. I beat him by a short head, but it's like the Ali v Louis argument. We can say and think what we like, or even get a computer to work it out, but in the end we still don't know. Bassi was at his peak and I was possibly close to mine, but we weren't on the bank together. End of story. I don't think there has ever been a head to head battle between two really good bleak anglers, certainly in our match angling history. I'd go a long way to see one, though!

The short pole, three sections with a standard (not flicktip) top, is the perfect weapon for bleak fishing, and this length is certainly required if you want a really big weight. A longer length is usable but more awkward, and by definition you are fishing too far out for one of the important functions in this job. It helps a lot to be able to see the fish, and the longer the pole the further you are away from them. Unshipping a section for even longer work just isn't on, unless you are really struggling to put together a few points in a hard team match.

Obviously the aim is to fish three sections to hand, i.e. the full length of line from pole tip to hook has to be almost as long as the pole. Find out by trial and error the exact length needed to swing a fish to the receiving hand without having to reach up or down for it. I use 3lb line with a hook length of $1^{1}/_{2}$ or 2lbs, usually with an 18 hook with the barb broken off to leave just a stump. Some anglers use eyed hooks to help prevent the bait - always maggot - from being blown up the line, but I don't do it that way. I settle for a fine wire, long shanked caster hook with a round bend, and there is a special way of putting the bait on it. Most readers will be aware of the way we put casters on the hook, putting the point into the thick end, and then pushing the caster round the bend and up the shank. That effectively buries the hook inside the caster, and for bleak fishing

I put a tough old maggot on in exactly the same way, bringing the hook point back out through the skin near the pointed end of the maggot (see Fig 39). You bump off a lot of bleak if you hook a maggot the conventional way. My method makes sure you hit a lot more of the bites, and it stops the bait being blown up the line.

The float depends on the situation, but for the big weights, which are usually taken in the top few inches of water, there is nothing

How the maggot is hooked for bleak fishing.

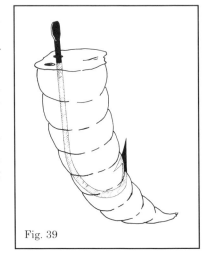

Fig. 39

*Italian international, Dino Bassi, pictured when he won the World Championship in
Italy in 1971. He also won in Bulgaria in 1976 with 384 fish in 90 minutes, and Tom
Pickering has dreamed of a bleak fishing encounter with Bassi ever since.*

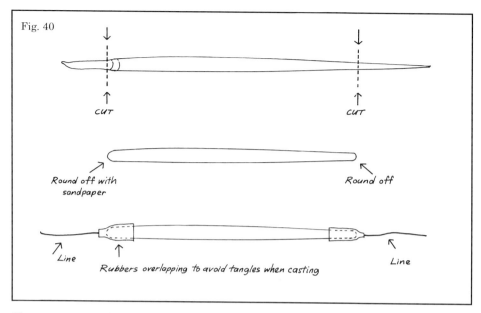

How a porcupine float is cut down to 2" in length, rounded off and rigged for bleaking.

to beat a short length of porcupine quill. I like to use a piece about two inches long, with the ends smoothed and rounded off. It is fished on the line about 3ft from the hook, fixed near both ends with tight silicone tubing overlapping the ends to prevent tangles (Fig 40). The 3ft length is critical. Any shorter and you miss too many fish, as I will explain later. If the conditions are right that's the entire rig - no shotting at all (Fig 41). I like the quill float because it has enough

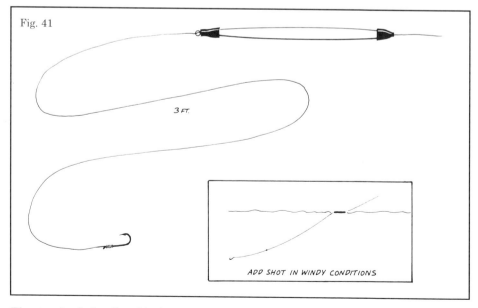

The standard, flat float bleak rigs. The line to the hook has to be about 3" long.

weight in it to cast, and it also lands with quite a splash. I think that helps to keep the bleak in the right spot, for when they are really on the feed they home in on the splashes of the bait as it hits the water. A somewhat bigger splash seems to turn them on even more.

Before I take you fishing with the rig, though, I will describe the rest of the tackle set-up, for literally everything has to be right. There's no rod rest, of course. The pole never leaves the hand throughout a match, but the placing of the keepnet is important. It has to be a wide-necked job set parallel to the water and touching your legs. Fish which drop off on the way in often have enough momentum to land in the net. Those which fall off late can hit the body and drop in. It is for this reason that some anglers fix up a "slide" - a piece of material rigged as a sort of extension to the bait apron, which runs down into the net. It channels in a few which might otherwise escape, but it is not something I have done.

The net I use is adjustable for height, and I like it fairly well above the water because of the preferred method of unhooking - flicking them off. It involves catching the line about two inches above the hook and simultaneously bending to take the fish a few inches below the rim of the net. At that point you flick the fish up and over in a sharp movement. Most of the time it will come off, but not always, and certainly not if it is hooked in the tough lower jaw. You have to learn how to recognise where the hook is as the fish is swinging towards you. If it is hooked in the lower jaw catch it, and unhook the conventional way. It may slow you down fractionally when a flicking operation doesn't work, but over five hours it's much faster.

Now that's out of the way, let's look more closely at the unshotted

Catching the line above the fish enables you to flick the catch straight into the net – sometimes!

Casting is a fast overarm movement, which takes float and maggot round in a circle and splashes them down hard on the water.

Throw a maggot in and count how long it takes to vanish into the mouth of a bleak.

porcupine quill rig. The casting method is important - a fast overarm movement which takes float and maggot round in a circle and splashes it all down hard on the water. When I first wrote about this method in Coarse Angler magazine I stressed the need for a very accurate cast, dropping the maggot very near to where the loose feed was going, but not among it. That was vital at that time, because the key to the method, and certainly to big weights, was to watch the hookbait. The float did not serve to signal bites (and still doesn't), for once the bleak feels resistance from this type of float it usually lets go. For that reason we were watching the maggot, assuming that when it disappeared a hungry mouth had closed over it. The obvious response was to strike. We have moved on from there since that advice appeared to a much better system, which covers the situations in which we can see the bleak and when we cannot see them.

It's a system based on counting, and when we can see the bleak it goes like this. Throw a maggot at them and count, noting how long it takes to vanish as a fish takes it. The timing can vary on different days, but let's assume that maggot disappeared on your count of four. You cast in with baited hook, count three and strike; that's one short of the original count, but there is a reason. The reaction time has to be accounted for. It will take you the extra time to think about striking, and for that action to take effect on the terminal tackle. You end up striking at the precise moment the bait is taken, and have the maximum chance of lifting that bleak before it can even think about ejecting the bait. I have simplified it a bit. You will find you need a short period of trial and error to get it exactly right, but it is quite easy, really. But how does it work when we cannot see the maggot, perhaps because of the light conditions, a bit of wave action or, maybe, a touch of colour in the water? You use the same system, really, but you have to find out the right time lapse by casting, counting and striking. Count three and strike, four and strike or whatever until you start to connect, though do not expect to come back with a fish every time. You can be striking 20 times a minute, catching from nothing to a dozen or so. What you are looking for, though, is an average of about two per minute overall. In five hours that's 600 bleak, and on the Trent that's 20lbs!

With the counting method casting accurately to the edge of the shoal is not required. The bait can go right among them, where the action is the most hectic. Just as important as where the tackle lands, though, is the way it lands. With a stick float you are trying to get it all to land in a straight line downstream, but with this approach you don't want it to land straight. The more in a heap it lands the better (Fig 42). That way a fish can swim quickly in any direction and I can strike before it begins to feel the weight of the float. A slight headwind helps it to land right, and so does the weight of the float. When it is going out ahead of a light hook the latter rarely carries on past the float to lie dead straight unless there is a wind to help it. That brings me to the next method, a slight variation of the first.

The tackle will tend to straighten if there's a slight ripple from an adverse wind, and the line will then start to bow between float and hook, which is even

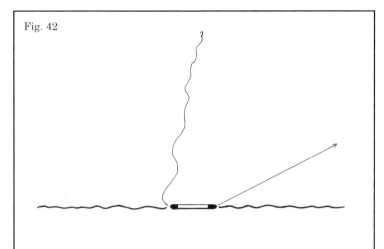

Fig. 42

When casting, try to make the line land in a heap, as indicated in these end-on and overhead illustrations

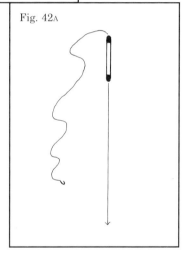

Fig. 42A

worse. The only way to conquer this problem is to get the line under with a small shot, a legal size 10 or 12, set 12 to 18" from the hook (see Fig 41 again). With this small amount of weight you can still fish in the top few inches, and both approaches are capable of producing large weights. Unfortunately bleak will not always make themselves available right up top, and strong winds can defeat both my favourite methods. An alternative approach is therefore required.

There are times when the bleak will not come high in the water, even when the conditions seem perfect. In this situation I used to retain the porcupine float but shot it like a stick float, with an evenly placed string of three or four No. 8 shots, terminating in a 10 set 12-18" from the hook. This rig would take the odd fish in the drop, but would get quite quickly to the depth where most of the fish were. It would catch anywhere from surface to the full depth, but it has now been replaced by a small bristle pole float, shotted in the same way as I've just described for the porcupine float. This approach (Fig. 43 overleaf) does the job in a much more efficient manner, as we've learned over the last few years by watching the Italians in the World Championship. When I use this method, with the shots strung out, I expect to catch bleak at different levels, but I am watching all the time for a pattern to emerge. It's a bit like stick float fishing, with the float first of all lying flat and then cocking in an orderly and predictable manner until the bait is taken. Then the float will behave in a slightly different way. It may stop cocking, pop up, tilt a bit or deviate in some other noticeable way from its normal setting. As well as watching for the bites, though, I am watching for some indication of exactly where the majority of those

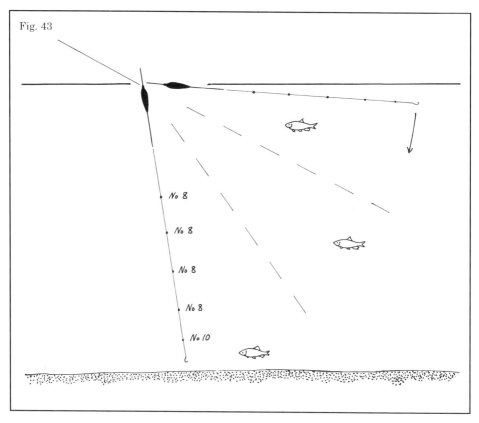

Fig. 43

No 8
No 8
No 8
No 8
No 10

FLOAT: GROUP B, .30g.
The bristle float rig for catching bleak at any depth, from surface to bottom.

bites are coming - 1ft down, 2ft or 3ft, a depth they rarely go below.

If the bites are mostly coming at one level I will then bunch the shot and adjust the float to drop the bait more rapidly to the exact level. All the shots will be placed together, only 3 to 4" from the hook (Fig 44), and providing you have got it right the catch rate will improve a great deal. The Italians are aces at this game, quickly finding the right level to fish the bait. They usually have several poles all rigged up ready for whatever they discover to be necessary, and they have invariably found out within 10 minutes. Nowadays their techniques and ours are very similar, except they use cloud groundbait to attract the bleak while we mostly loose feed.

Generally speaking it is strong winds which keep the bleak well below the surface, and that can prove too awkward for the flat float methods and the pole float. In these circumstances we need to switch to a miniature waggler float set-up. Originally I used either a small sarcandas reed float or a small upside down crowquill (thin end uppermost), locked on the line with a couple of no, 8 shots. Both would still do the job, though now I use a small canal crystal float taking about 2 no 4 overall (Fig 45). It has a nice, fine insert in the tip, and is perfect for the job. The tactics are the same as they are with the pole float, but we lose some of the efficiency. Even so, it is possible to take weights well into double figures if the bleak are sizable and the shoal is big.

All four of the methods described are usually fished 3ft deep, but the pole float rig with the stick float shotting has proved a useful one in winter league fishing when set to fish the full depth of a swim. It catches bleak and the odd bonus fish of other species, and many times it has helped the Barnsley team to score vital section points.

Now all the float rigs have been described, and one or two bits of the technique, I will return to the original unshotted surface catching tackle and take you on a fishing session with it. It will be not be an imaginary match, but a real one, the Shelford event which Denis

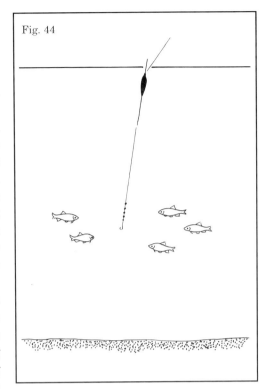

Fig. 44

FLOAT; GROUP B, .30g.
If bleak are feeding at one depth, bunch the shots like this.

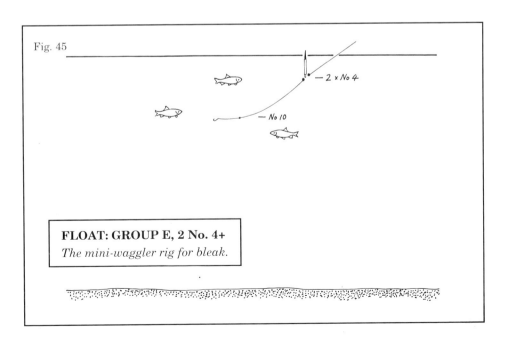

Fig. 45

— 2 x No 4

— No 10

FLOAT: GROUP E, 2 No. 4+
The mini-waggler rig for bleak.

White still thinks I blew. I was in two minds on the trip to the Trent as to what to go for. The conditions seemed right for a good catch of anything, and I only bleak fish in open events if I think it can win. I never, ever, aim for just a place in a match. I'm there to win, and much of the preceding week is devoted to thinking out the right method to do just that.

On this occasion I wasn't sure, not even after the draw. The trouble with bleak is that they tend to like the same kind of swims as roach and other species. Despite the fact that they feed up in the water much of the time they actually seem to like a nice, even bottom and a smooth flow with no surface boils. I drew such a swim, and with no immediate sign of bleak activity I tried the stick float for roach. Normally if the bleak are in the mood to come up top they show it fairly quickly, and that's when you have to make the decision whether or not to go for them. In a situation which gets many anglers grumbling that they cannot get through the bleak we immediately go for them instead. As I said in the Coarse Angler articles back in 1977 there is no point in figuring out how to get through 30lbs of bleak to reach a stone of roach!

At Shelford, though, I was catching neither species, and it was 95 minutes into the match when I first saw a bleak break the surface. Then there was a few minutes' thinking time, plus the time it took to set the pole up - two minutes, maybe. I started to feed loose maggots reasonably heavily to try and get the bleak more interested and to get them closer together. I put in about 20 maggots three times a minute for a while, hoping to bring more in from further downstream.

Feeding correctly is the real key to match fishing success, and that "maggot a second" average is something which must not be kept up for too long. Once the bleak are shoaled up and boiling on the top I cut down to 12, fed three times a minute. That's just about enough to keep them there, and all the maggots are scoffed before they can drop downstream. Offer too many and the bleak will simply follow them, and it takes time to get them back into the right place. Sometimes they won't come back at all. Do it right and the shoal is yours for as long as you want them, but at Shelford they were none too keen, initially.

My normal target is to catch 100 in the first hour, and build it up from there. On this occasion I got only 60, and was struggling for a variety of reasons. The wind was gusting about and making it a bit awkward, and it seemed that every time I got them together a boat came along. Boats are deadly for bleak, even if they are well out in mid river. Big barges actually make the river go the other way, briefly, and even the smaller craft - especially those coming upstream - cause some sort of minor flow change which helps to scatter the bleak. They know a boat is coming before we do, and the bites tail off. There may well be a case for going in with a stick float rig to fish the depth when a boat is coming. The odd bonus fish could weigh more than the bleak we catch from a boat-disturbed swim. However, back to the problems I was having. The last and possibly the worst was that I was rusty, not having fished for bleak since the previous autumn.

I had checked my watch on several occasions, and that's vital too. I have to know whether the catch rate is good enough to win, and I was just about concluding that it wasn't when the rate started to pick up. I had five minute spells when I was catching 14 per minute, interspersed with periods when I would catch only 10 in five minutes, but it was building up nicely. Switching from tough bronze maggot to equally tough whites began to improve things in the slower spells. You need real leathery bait for this game. Fresh maggots are smashed much too easily, and you are changing too often.

Anyway, the catch rate accelerated and I started to get a much smoother rhythm going. High speed bleaking isn't a frantic thrash with all the nerve ends jangling. It's a smooth, relaxed exercise demanding intense concentration, rather than sheer physical effort. If you make the conscious effort to go faster you will get slower instead. I used to think that bleak bite faster in the early part of a match, and more slowly later, until I eventually realised that it was me getting more relaxed as the rhythm and style improved.

Maintaining an even pace and rhythm is quite difficult, though. You might want it but the bleak don't. They come and go, and that breaks your rhythm. Gusting wind has the same effect, and the odd boat wrecks everything for a few minutes. Without intense concentration you are sunk, and my way of maintaining it in matches is to both count the fish and to time myself. I set myself targets. That 100 fish in the first hour is a standard I set myself when I first started, but I've had as many as 250. Averaging 200 to 250 and hour throughout a match is good going, and I think I ended up with about 700 at Shelford, mostly taken in the last $2^1/_2$ hours.

I suppose I must have done around 300 in my best hour but I was a bit surprised when they went over 22lbs. I hadn't felt I was fishing well, and I made a mental note to polish up my techniques. I tried to do this in practice sessions, but that Shelford match was actually the last in which I had the chance to put together a good bleak weight. I got a big reputation as the "Bionic Bleaker" on the strength of just two performances of around three hours in actual matches and that one 35lb return in practice at Collingham.

I don't really miss the bleak now, for as I said in the beginning, I never really liked this way of fishing. What I do regret, though, is not being able to fully polish the technique for a method I obviously had a talent for. I carry this mental image of Dino Bassi in Bulgaria, based on a conversation I had with Colin Dyson after he came back. I asked him what Bassi had actually looked like on the way to that world title. The answer amounted to my idea of the ultimate bleak angler.

"He's a sawn-off little man, but quick as a cat, without actually looking hurried," he said. "He fished sitting down, I think because the water was clear and he wanted his fish as close in as possible without scaring them. His casting action was that of a metronome; an automaton, or as near to that as a human being can get. He had his fish off the hook so fast I couldn't quite see how he did it, and he seemed to catch a hell of a lot of bleak before having to change his bait.

It's hard to imagine how a taller man with much longer arms could achieve the same smooth style. He was brilliant, Tom."

And I'd always thought that being tall with long arms gave me an edge!

The writer with his 22lb bleak catch, taken in three hours from the Trent at Shelford.

COPING WITH CARP

by Tom Pickering

I want to devote a separate section to this rather exciting exercise because it makes a number of important points about pole handling, the playing of fish and the way elastic does its job. Landing a good carp is the ultimate challenge for the pole angler, and it can be done with the right techniques and a bit of patience. One thing I never do is criticise or make fun of other anglers and their methods. Instead I try to understand why they do what they do, and work out whether any of it is relevant to the way I fish for their species in the match fishing context. What interests me most about carp anglers are the techniques they use to fool carp into taking their baits. The two contrasting approaches are to make them feel a heavy weight and bolt, or to deceive them with ultra sensitive tactics. I don't think bolt rigs have any application in match fishing except maybe when we are legering for carp. On the pole, and with the emphasis on finesse, we have to look at the other approach - deception.

Carp have a reputation for learning about the different methods of bait presentation where specialist anglers fish for them with heavy gear, and I am sure they also learn on waters where they are the regular quarry of matchmen. The Shillamill fishery in Cornwall is a good example. I have enjoyed the festival events there, and had a good bit of success, but I don't think I would have done so well had I assumed that any pole fishing approach would work. I soon noticed, for example, that with a big pole float I wasn't getting any bites. I saw the odd bob and dip, but nothing developed, and for a while I assumed it was the odd fish brushing the line. In the end I tumbled to the fact that I had carp in the swim, and the tiny float movements had been caused by carp testing the tackle. They were feeling for resistance, and even though it cannot have been much it was enough! As soon as I switched to a light pole float I got proper bites and caught some carp.

You have to compromise in the finesse department when you are after carp. For almost all my pole fishing I use fine wire hooks, size 26 to 22 being used most often, but for carp, or where good tench are likely, I go to forged 22 or 20 hooks. The line is usually 3lb, with a 1.7lb hook length, and while the big carp boys might laugh at the idea that's heavy for me. I've lost my finesse in every department except one. I can still use a small and lightly shotted float taking,

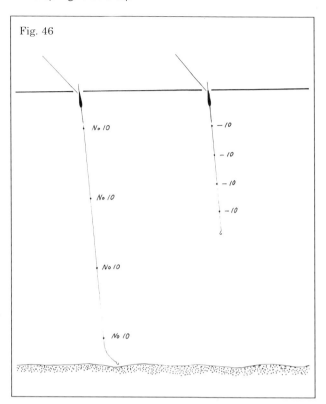

Fig. 46

FLOAT: GROUP C, .10g.

Light tackle rigs catch carp when heavier tackle won't – and don't be afraid to try for them in mid-water as well as on the bottom.

say, four no. 10 shots strung out (Fig 46). That tiny float, slightly overshotted even with four 10s, is held up by that little dodge with the grease I mentioned earlier. No carp, however crafty, can test the bait on that tackle without giving me an indication I can strike at. You have got to get the bites, or nothing else I say here about carp will mean a thing to anyone.

An important factor in achieving bites is the old and obvious one - to present the bait in the right way, and in the right place. Spend some time watching carp and you will see them patrolling at virtually any level, from surface to bottom. With a light float shotted for a slow falling bait you can get a bite at any level. At Shillamill, and other places where I have fished for them, they tend to patrol the near bank, working their way along the ledges, and stopping for a snack wherever they find loose feed, whether it is falling past them or on the bottom. On some pegs the ledge is only three metres from the bank, and I don't need to emphasise the fact that with three metres of pole in your hand, and a good carp at the other end you have a problem or two to sort out. The carp will go zooming off into the lake at a fair old pace, and even if you have chosen the right grade of elastic a decent carp can make mincemeat of it on the first run. The elastic needs a bit of help, and all we can do is ship the pole - i.e. add some sections to the three you have in your hand. It pays to have the spare sections already laid out behind you, and in a position where you can get hold of them in the right sequence, without really looking.

116

As you add sections you are feeding the pole to the carp, effectively slowing down what it can take out of the elastic. You have to keep on doing it until the carp's first run is under control. That is the number one priority. That carp's first run has to be stopped, and if you don't manage that it's goodbye. You might wind up with 7, 8, or nine metres of pole, maybe even more, but more often than not carp in single figures and sometimes into double figures will be stopped. By adding sections you are effectively increasing the area in which the carp can swim, and when that first hectic rush is over you have a great chance of landing it, providing there are no bad snags it can dive into.

It won't be yours in a hurry, though. It will swim round and round in circles in front of you, seemingly for ages, but gradually it seems to work itself up towards the top. It won't give in. Carp never do that, but after a while the elastic will take the steam out of it and slow it down. The runs get shorter and slower, and as you realise that is happening you can then start to think about feeding some pole back through your hands and unshipping, section by section. Just think about it, though. Do not actually do it at that stage. Wait until the carp is obviously ready. If it's not you will spook it, and it will start dashing around again.

You have to have your wits about you from the moment the fish is first hooked, and respond in a smooth and efficient way, particularly when you are lengthening the pole. Don't even do that in a frantic hurry. Add a section when it is obvious that you need to. Don't go clapping on section after section in a sort of blind panic. Your aim is to keep control of that carp, so take note of the effect the addition of each section is having. It's a bit like playing a fish on rod and reel. You backwind only when you have to and for as long as you have to. If you don't the fish ends up under control, but a long way away, and it has to come all the way back. Exactly the same thing happens when you add sections to the pole. You can end up jamming 11 metres together when 9 or even 7 metres might have done. For a while, at least, you are stuck with playing a lively carp on the full length of pole, and it can be very tiring. That's just for starters. With 11 metres up the distance with stretched elastic is incredible; the area the carp can swim around in is vast.

The best way is to make your mind up when you do hook a carp to add just one section, then watch the elastic stretching. It will be obvious if it needs another section, and if it does you add one, and watch again. Let the carp tell you when another section is needed. Don't just assume it needs another two or three. If you add them too rapidly you have taken nothing out of the carp. Make it work for every section you give it. That way, and only that way, will you end up playing the fish out on the shortest possible length of pole. The idea is to make it hard for the fish - not hard for yourself! I can remember watching the Nottingham matchman Jan Porter playing a 7lb carp in the Trent, and he had clapped too many sections on. I think he got to 11 metres, and realised he could have stopped it on 9 metres. It took Jan ages to land that carp, and he wound up absolutely knackered.

The two carp which were stretching the elastic when the pictures were taken for the "Choice of Elastics" chapter and the front cover – proof that the methods described here really work!

You might think it's easy to remove a couple of sections if you think you have put too many on, but it doesn't work like that. When the fish is first stopped, be it at 11 metres or 9, it is still very lively, and you can't start feeding the pole back and taking off sections. All you can do is hold on and wait while it does its circular tour of the swim, and that seems to be a hard job for some anglers. Sitting there for five minutes, just holding on and letting the carp swim against the elastic, seems like half an hour, but you have got be be patient. Those who lose patience, and try to haul the carp in, are the ones who end up losing them. I will sit it out for as long as it takes for that carp to work its way to the top. It's then, and only then, when you can get the fish coming towards you and take the opportunity to remove some sections. I cannot stress too much the importance of choosing the right moment to try and net the fish. Some anglers try it when they see the carp about a foot below the surface, but it isn't ready then. If they try at that stage to get it coming towards them the extra pressure applied can pull the hook out. I think what happens is that as the carp fights its circular battle the angle of pull on the hook is constantly changing, and the hook-hold is gradually wearing out. Undue pressure in the later stages can then pull it out, whereas with a little more patience, and a bit less pressure, the hook will hold for just long enough.

I love this method of fishing. I find it tremendously exciting, but you have to realise the limitations. One of the lakes at Shillamill has carp in it which are too big for the elastic to cope with, and I usually fish the rod and reel there. They can be hooked at close range again, but having learned the lesson of the light float I simply use that on the rod and reel tackle. Obviously it is too light to cast any distance, so I just flick it in as far as I can beyond the rod end. Fish a normal waggler for those carp, and you get the little bobs and dips that come to nothing. At short range with the small pole float you can sometimes see carp coming along, and quite often the float is away seconds later.

Lessons learned in one game are often relevant to another! It is perhaps a good moment to make the point that everything I have said about carp is also applicable to tench. They are shy fish which will take a bait more readily on light tackle, and once hooked they are dealt with in more or less the same way. Obviously you can stop them quicker, play them out on a shorter length of pole, but really it's just carp fishing in miniature, and just as much fun.

SO YOU WANT
TO CATCH EELS

by Tom Pickering

Many people don't, of course! Dick Walker's famous crack that anyone writing a book on how not to catch eels would make a small fortune would strike a chord with a lot of anglers, including many matchmen, but not this one! I'm in the opposite camp, and a substantial number of match anglers are right there with me. There are some, I suspect, who will buy this book for this chapter alone. Eels, for those who can catch them, are often matchwinners, and I love catching them. If there was a venue where eels made up the winning catches from June to September that's where I would be every week, without fail. Eels are a major challenge, and that's the kind of fishing I like. They make me think. It's a busy method. Five hours fly by like five minutes on a river like the Witham, which for me presents the most intriguing and difficult eel fishing a match angler is ever likely to encounter.

Nobody pegged near me on the Witham would suspect that I love what I am doing. Those eels have me cussing and swearing every few minutes. They are the only fish which make me miss more bites than I hook, and they seem to be unique. I have this vision of a mass migration of eels from the Sargasso. They stop in the South West Approaches for IQ tests, and all those in the A-level class are directed to the River Witham. The brainless ones go everywhere else. Eels are a lot easier wherever else I fish for them, though why this should be so I cannot imagine. On places like the Welland I can hit nearly every bite, but on the Witham it's one in three or four - and that's on the good days! I do not think anyone does better than that, but anyone who can take a winning weight of eels on the Witham can do it anywhere. Fish badly for them on the Witham and the missed bite ratio will be one in 10 to one in 20.

I am not noted as a defeatist, but after devoting many hours on the banks of the Witham, and many more just thinking about the problems those eels present, I do not think it is possible to do any better than one in three. If you don't think so, right now, you will at the end of this chapter! I will break you in gently with a description of the tackle, starting with the pole end system. Some anglers use flicktip, but for me it has to be elastic. Hook a big one with a flicktip and it will be hard to get it up off the bottom. It will just tear off and smash you, but with elastic they are beaten for all the same reasons mentioned earlier in this book. They run fast and stretch the elastic, but it soon takes the steam out of them. I use no. 5 elastic, fixed a bit tighter than it is for other species. Not too tight. Even the smaller ones have to be able to take some elastic out, for if they don't you will bump some off that would otherwise be caught.

The rig itself is 2lb main line, 1lb hook length and either a 22 or a 24 barbless hook. It has to be a small hook, because you need them to take it right into their mouths. They tend to take the bait in funny ways, sometimes grabbing the maggot sideways. They have less chance of having the hook if it's a big one, and I reckon a lot of the bites we miss are down to the eel taking that maggot sideways with the hook still outside the mouth. When we strike we feel the bump, then nothing. You haven't had the slightest chance of hooking the eel. The reason why it has to be a barbless hook is dealt with later, but the pattern is a Mustad 90340. It's not a heavy hook, but it is strong enough to hold the fish and not to bend when you are unhooking it.

The float has to be the lightest you can get away with, and I never use an olivette. The normal, standard float will take half a gramme, but if the water is running through I would have to go heavier, up to $1\frac{1}{2}$ grammes. In a wind, and no flow, it might have to be threequarter of a gramme, but I always want the lightest I can control. If there is little or no flow it would be a stillwater float, but with some run on the river I will use the smaller of the round-bodied floats. Colour of the bristle is important, for reasons which will soon emerge. It must not be black. It has to be blaze or yellow - colours which can be seen when the float is under the water.

The shotting pattern is a no. 10 a foot from the hook, with an 8 a foot above that. About a foot to 18 inches above the eight I usually bunch three or four number 6s, depending on the size of the float. The float is set to fish about six inches of line on the bottom (Fig 47).

FLOATS: GROUP C (water still), .50g, or GROUP B (moving water), .75g.

The preferred eel tackle for the River Witham, set 6" over depth. (For variations see text).

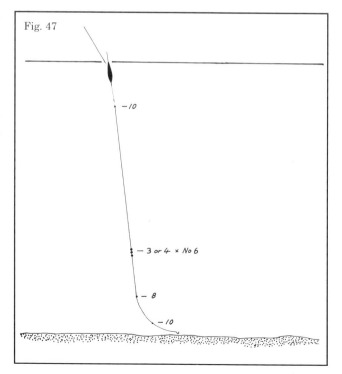

Fig. 47

-10

$- 3$ or $4 \times$ No 6

$- 8$

$- 10$

Eels played a vital part in the writer's Macpherson UK Championship victory in 1988. This was a section winning catch on the Coronation Channel.

That's as heavy as I want to fish for eels, for the heavier you fish the more bites you will miss!

That's all straightforward, up to now, but what is really complicated is the feeding of the swim and the bites. For a start I try and feed two lines, because I don't know where the eels are going to be. I always feed the near ledge, which is usually about five metres out, and then another line at 11 metres. You don't want the two swims too close. If the ledge was at 8 metres, say, you could not feed 11 metres, for the two swims would just about join up. You would have to go longer than 11 metres if you had a long enough pole, but luckily the near ledge is around five metres. Fishing at five and 11 is usually about right.

You might never get to fish on the near line, but if and when you do catch close you are on for a big weight. Most of the really good eel weights come from the Pound Length, where the near ledge is very close in. I always trickle some feed in on the near line just in case they decide to feed there, but mainly it's a reserve option if the far swim dies, or if I want to rest it for a while. You can usually pick off a few in the near swim, but the far line is generally the critical one. I always begin by fishing the 11 metre line, and I always rig the tackle so I am fishing the last five metres to hand. It does not matter about fishing a short line from pole tip to float with this method. In fact it is a positive advantage to have a bit more, as you will see. Some of the bites are so sudden and violent they will pull on the pole tip if the line is too short. Fortunately the depth at 11 metres on the Witham is such that with the last five metres to hand, you usually have 3 to 4ft of line to the float. That is about right for some of the tricks we have to employ to hit the bites.

The system of feeding is critical. Not as much goes into the near line as the far one, and I always keep a close eye on how much I am putting in. In the course of a match I try to get rid of about two pints of maggots. Much more than that and you are probably overdoing it for eels, if they are feeding well. It may sound strange, but it's on the days when they are not feeding well that you get rid of a lot of feed. Some days I find I have thrown five pints, which takes a bit of explaining, but I will try. You might throw a little handful at the start and get a bite straight away. In the first five or ten minutes you should then get bites fairly regularly, and if you are you simply carry on with that rate of feed. The only time you have to feed more heavily is when you are not getting bites. You have to feed, feed feed until you get them into the swim, but once they are there you do not have to feed so many.

Feed heavily when they are either not there or not feeding, just to get them going. But if they are there and feeding at the start you have to go really steady, and if they have fed all through the match you should have got rid of two pints - that's about 20 to 25 maggots every cast. On the near line the feeding rate should be half that, maybe 10 a time. Over-feeding in the early stages is the biggest mistake many anglers make, and it is understandable, in a way. With other species we often try to step up the catch rate by increasing the feed, but with eels that can be fatal. If you have 5lbs of eels in front of you then you have to catch 5lbs, but you won't if you overdo the feeding. I have caught 12lbs of eels on two pints of maggots, and have rarely had to use three pints.

The actual method of bait presentation is not difficult. I just cast in and try to hold the bait still on the bottom. The Witham is still most of the time in summer, or has a slight draw on it. If there is a bit of movement I let it work on the tackle, pulling it through very slowly. It doesn't seem to matter to the eels whether the bait is still or moving slightly, though on the odd day when it might be running off more quickly I then try to hold the bait back, as still as I can. If there's an awkward wind blowing the float has to be well-controlled, for if the tackle is dragging all over the place that does affect your chances of attracting bites. I little bit of float movement doesn't matter, for with six inches of line on the bottom it won't move the bait. On the odd occasion, just to contradict myself a bit, it can sometimes pay to let the wind bounce the float along if you aren't getting any action. Now and again it can provoke an eel to feed, but the general rule is to keep the bait as still as possible.

Now we have finally reached the really tricky bit - those bites! Sometimes, usually quite early in a match, you might get the odd bite on the drop, and for some reason I mostly hit those. The majority, however, come after the float has cocked and settled. It then disappears in the usual manner, but if you strike straight away you will miss it - that's virtually guaranteed. You have to watch the float under the water (hence the need for coloured tips) or the line above the float. If it's a rapid bite with the line zooming off down the same hole as the float I count slowly to four and strike. Most of the time these are hooked - they are what we call the kamikaze bites, and they are quite easy.

Unfortunately these bites are almost as rare as retired kamikaze pilots! Much more common is the bite which slowly takes the float under the surface and holds there for a couple of seconds. You can see the bristle, as a rule, but you have to resist the temptation to strike. Just watch, instead. After two or three seconds the float will come back up, and then it starts going again. You have to watch as it goes slowly down into the water. If you lose sight of the float you have to switch attention to the line, to see if it is still following the float down into the water. Then you strike, and you might hit the eel. Strike any earlier and you almost never will connect with that type of bite. It is no use striking and casting all the time, more in hope than expectation.

There is one type of bite you never hit at all, and that's the one which takes the float slowly down to four inches below the surface, where it holds. It goes no further and does not come up. Don't wait for anything else to happen, because it won't. Just strike, miss and drop back in again. These bites, I am sure, are caused by the tiny little eels about the size of lobworms. You won't hook them so pull the bait away from them and start again. If you start to get a lot of these bites then you should step up the feeding rate to try and feed them off. You don't want to waste your time on eels of this size, so fill them up and try to attract bigger eels with the additional feed. It's another reason why you have to carry five pints of maggots, when you only want to use two.

Concentrate on the other types of bite – the odd one on the drop, the fast runaway and the down, up and down again variety. You will not hit more than one in three, even by doing everything I have said so far, but there is more. Part of the system with all these bites is to move the pole tip over the spot where the float was, immediately it goes down (Fig. 48). It creates some slack line and reduces the chance of a fast bite registering on the pole tip. It also reduces resistance, and allows you to watch the slack line following the float. All this underlines why it pays to have the longer length between pole tip and float for eel fishing.

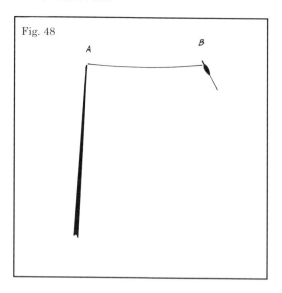

Fig. 48

A

B

When an eel bite develops waste no time in moving the pole tip from point A to point B.

When you do hook an eel don't bother playing it. I don't even bother to watch what is happening. I immediately feed the pole back six metres, and unship at the five metre length. During this stage I leave the elastic to do its job. It will be stretching as I feed back, particularly if I have hooked a good one. An especially big eel might still be more or less where it was when I started to feed the pole back, though with the average eel the elastic will have stretched about six feet by the time I raise the five metre length of pole. It will then come to the surface as the elastic beats it, and the next step is to decide whether to swing it in to hand or net it. Over 3oz I always net them, even though such a weight or even much bigger can be swung. I net them because of their habit of lashing around and twisting themselves into knots. When they writhe up and straighten even small eels can break the line, but they don't ball themselves up in the water quite so much.

I always have the keepnet right in front of me and fairly high above the water for eel fishing. The reason is that when I swing a small eel I bring it right into the top of the net and grab it from the outside of the net. The mesh gives me a good grip, and I can look to see where the hook is. If it is visible I unhook in the normal way, but being barbless the hook comes out with no trouble. A barbed hook, even one with a micro-barb, takes some removing from the tough mouth of an eel, and very often you end up bending the hook. If the hook is out of sight I break off. Other species of fish are easily and safely unhooked, wherever the hook is, but I think you can damage an eel poking around with a disgorger. The mouth is so small and its grip on the disgorger is so tight. So is our grip on the slippery fish itself. For one reason or another eels won't allow safe removal of

A small eel on the pole helps to keep the catch rate going in a Macpherson UK Championship round on the Grand Union Canal.

a hook lodged inside their mouths, but specialist anglers tell us that eels can get rid of hooks if they are left alone. If I net an eel I unhook the same way, using the mesh once again to grip the eel. When it is unhooked I take the head of the net inside the keepnet and tip it in. Any other way you risk losing it!

I always carry about 50 hooks ready tied for eel fishing, for obvious reasons, and it is very important to have enough. If you are fishing for, say, 10lbs of eels on the Witham you are talking about 60-plus fish, and you will lose quite a few hooks on that lot. Another sensible precaution is to check your keepnet for holes, because if there is one, anywhere, the eels will surely find it. I check my net the night before, the morning of the match and again on the river bank, but even then I have been known to miss one. It is agonising the lift what you think is a netful of eels, only to find nothing but a hole, ringed with slime, where your catch has wriggled free. It cost me second place, at least, in one Witham open, and at Barnsley we actually train people to check their nets. Even then it has cost us valuable points in team events.

Getting them into the net in the first place is the biggest problem, though, and as you will have gathered by now it's quite a challenge. I have described the different types of bites, and what the response should be, but I have probably under-stated the difficulties. At times the sheer number of missed bites drives you crazy, and it can be particularly bad in the last hour. I think the reason for this may be that bigger eels have moved into the swim. I like to catch 2 to 4oz eels, and with them hitting one in four or one in three bites is quite possible, if you follow the advice I have given. But the bigger eels of around 10oz to $1^1/_4$lbs are a nightmare, so much so I would not want them in the swim, given a choice.

The reason I think many of the missed bites are from big eels is that after missing bite after bite after bite, and you eventually connect with one, it is usually a big one. Often it will have a real mouthful of maggots, and I think that is the key to the problem. The small eels may take three or four maggots one after the other, mostly picked up sideways, but then they will have to stop to swallow them. The bigger eels seem to go around picking up about 20 or more in the same way, and if it clamps onto the hookbait and swims off to find another maggot it is going to register a bite which is almost impossible to strike correctly.

It is that knowledge which enables me to accept something I will not find acceptable in any other form of fishing. There is usually a solution to missed bites, either in the shotting or in the way a bait is presented, but not with eels on the Witham. I know I will hit only one third of the bites at best, and that there is nothing more I can do about it. Anybody who says he can hit most of them is telling little pork pies. The secret is to hit more than most other anglers, and if you study the match results you will see which anglers are managing to do that. It's a rather select band of men based mostly locally, in Kirkstead and Lincoln. They have done endless homework on the problem, and so have my Barnsley team-mates. What nobody can understand, though, is why eels are easier everywhere else.

GROUNDBAIT MIXES

by Tom Pickering

Do they work, these fancy and expensive groundbait mixes we buy from the likes of Sensas, Van den Eynde and the rest? It's a short question which is often put to me, in the shop and on the roadshows, and it could be a long answer. The short response is yes, they do. Products which con anglers have a short shelf life, and many of these mixes were on sale on the Continent for many years before they ever came here. Anglers over there are no less sceptical and penny-pinching than they are here.

Our forefathers were using a variety of different flavours in their groundbaits in the last century, but for some reason it died out in more modern times. Billy Lane was virtually alone in recommending aniseed in groundbait in his era, but it was one of the few things he advocated which did not catch on. More recently the import of Continental mixes coincided both with the rise in popularity of pole fishing and publicity for the boilie method of carp fishing.

The carp lads proved beyond doubt that their flavours and smells attracted carp, and they also stumbled across certain products which were rather too effective, from their point of view, in attracting other species of fish. That is when the more receptive ears in the match fishing fraternity began to tune in to what was happening. It gave us yet another problem to sort out - which of the mixes and products were relevant to us? It's a vast field for research, with a maze in the middle!

I decided at an early stage not to get too involved. I could see too many blind alleys I might wind up in. The biggest blind alley of all is the notion that magic groundbaits could become a substitute for both the luck of the draw and skill. It is also very difficult to establish beyond reasonable doubt whether a particular catch would have been just as big, or maybe even bigger, if ordinary bread crumb had been used instead.

Another problem, and it is something my co-author Colin Dyson can vouch for, is that a certain mix can eliminate some of the fish you need to catch. I gave him a recipe which had caught lots of skimmer bream for me - half Sensas Magic, half ordinary breadcrumb, a handful of bleak groundbait (Record 515) to make the mix cloud a bit and a bag of Sensas Tonic (vanilla). He and his mate Dave Beaumont used it in club matches on a lake, and nobody ever out-caught them when it came to small skimmers. Sometimes they were the only anglers to catch them in any quantity, but they still weren't winning. They got a lot of high places, but were always beaten by anglers with catches of bream in the 12oz to $1\frac{1}{2}$lb class, or with the 2 to 4oz skimmers they were catching plus a few of the better bream. Colin and Dave never caught those bonus fish, and the penny dropped with them one day when Colin got a lot of line bites leading to a foulhooked bream and a similarly foulhooked crucian carp.

He came to see me. "That Magic mix..." he said. "Don't use it any more," I said. "Yes, and I bet I know why," he replied. "It's pulling better bream into the swims but they won't have it when they get there. Our catches look like they came from different waters to the weights which have been beating us!"

He was right, and he actually sorted that out quicker then me. I'd been mostly using it on a water where all the skimmer bream were small, and it was only when I tried it on other waters with a bigger size range that I realised what was wrong. That mix remains an excellent one for small skimmer waters, and for some reason it will also catch skimmers of the size Colin couldn't catch if they are the smallest bream in the water. It's no good, though, if you are eliminating the chance of catching the bigger fish.

How many other mixes are there which achieve the same effect? It is so easy to conclude that a mix is good because it is catching, but you also have to ask yourself what it isn't catching. My rule of thumb is that if a mix is catching a representative sample of the fish the water is known to hold then at least it isn't doing any harm. Whether it is actually helping you is a matter for longer-term assessment, but very often the verdict is positive.

Apart from the basic bloodworm approach already described my use of groundbait is virtually restricted to bream and gudgeon fishing, and I will often use the bloodworm method for bream if I can. There are places where bloodworm is banned, of course, and I then have to look at a groundbait, caster and/or maggot approach. When we discovered the problems with the original Magic mix I had to experiment to find out which of the ingredients was putting off the bigger bream. I eventually found that it wasn't the Magic, and that if it was used without the Tonic and the bleak groundbait it was a lot less selective in its effect. I was catching the bigger bream as well as the skimmers.

That was in the days before we began to see the merits of wet leam, so the basic bream mix now is one third Magic, one third damp leam and one third bread crumb groundbait - the bloodworm mixture without the bloodworm, and mixed in much the same way. It is perhaps be a bit wetter and tackier, though maybe it simply comes out that way because of the absence of the bloodworm and the dry leam used to separate it. I load it with caster, maggot or both and feed four to six big balls at the start, topping up later, if necessary, with smaller balls.

If the water I am fishing holds mostly small skimmers the mix changes. I will take out most or all the leam and replace it with Tonic which, as you will have gathered earlier, really turns on small bream. This mixes up softer and lighter

Just a few samples from what can seem to be a baffling selection of continental groundbait mixes.

and I cloud it into the swim, drip-feeding it every cast. It's a nice, busy way of fishing which I find very enjoyable.

After several years of use, though, I have lately found that the Magic appears to be losing some of its appeal on waters where it has been used a lot. It happens a lot quicker for carp anglers, apparently. They find some baits last longer than others, but eventually they all get "blown," as they put it. I think we are beginning to see the same effect with our smaller and supposedly "less intelligent" fish.

Anyway, I realised I had to find something different, but which worked just as well, eventually settling for Van den Eynde's Super Cup. This has a sort of chocolate smell, and it seems to work as an all-round bait. As a cloud it works very well indeed, for bream of mixed sizes, and it is also an excellent bait for gudgeon. They really like it. I use it in exactly the same way, with the same extra ingredients, as the Magic.

Although I have praised Super Cup for gudgeon I would not use it if I was after gudgeon only, though that is entirely because Sensas Picardie is even better for this species. It has a sort of curry smell which really attracts and holds them in the swim. It catches other species too, but up to now I have not found a superior bait for gudgeon fishing.

Don't ask me for a groundbait mix for roach, because I do not honestly believe there is one which is more effective than simple loose-feeding with maggot or caster. I will obviously use the bloodworm approach for roach, but they are not interested in the mix which carries the bloodworm to them. They only want the bloodworms themselves, so nothing is lost in using groundbait in that situation. Even so, if roach are the only species present I will play safe and use bloodworm and joker much more neat, as described in the bloodworm chapter. Groundbait used with maggot or caster, however, simply turns them off, though we cannot rule out the possibility that somebody will, some day, come up with something which will switch them on.

Chub are another species for which groundbait is usually poison, and a fortune awaits anyone who can resolve that situation. All my groundbaiting, apart from with bloodworm, is aimed exclusively at bream and gudgeon, and I don't think I go too far wrong. As to what goes in it, I'd say casters and some pinkies for bigger bream. I'm not a fan of squatts except when I'm fishing soft cloud for small skimmers. I have a thing about pinkies, even when I am loose feeding with big maggots or casters. I nearly always drop in the odd handful of pinkies, which are a great bait for quality roach.

Actually mixing groundbait requires some observations. The amount of water used determines the consistency, and it's a question of experimenting to find out what is best for your own waters. Generally speaking it has to go down and break up quickly for bigger bream, and cloud down for the smaller fish. Mix the ingredients thoroughly while dry, and then add the mix to the water - never the other way around. And when you have mixed with the water there is a vast improvement in the texture and quality if the mix is then rubbed through a riddle.

I learned that many years ago from the writings of Billy Lane who, I'm told, had to mix his father's breadcrumb groundbait when he was a lad. He had to do it the night before a match, and woe betide him if it had any lumps in it. He avoided a clip round the ear by rubbing it through a maggot riddle. Groundbait mixed overnight and used next day is much better than a bankside mix for immediate use - if you can manage to carry it! There is more time for the moisture to permeate every particle, so it's really consistent. It squeezes together beautifully, and how hard you do that dictates to some extent whether it goes down and breaks up, or breaks up on the way down. For the latter job, however, I will mix with more water, which makes it better still. With bankside mixes, however, rubbing it through a riddle gets the bait a long way towards the quality of an overnight mix. It is well worth spending that bit of extra time on it.

I haven't mentioned any other types of groundbait, simply because I haven't used them yet. Hand on heart, I have mentioned every mix I currently use, but that does not mean others are not as good or even better. My advice is to experiment and to find something you can have every confidence in. Stick fairly closely to my proportions, one third breadcrumb, one third wet leam, one third continental, and you won't be far of the mark in terms of mixing quality.

One problem many anglers have is deciphering the packets which continental groundbaits come in. Some are not yet printed in English, though I understand that is in the pipeline. To help readers with their experiments, therefore, I have asked the leading firms to nominate their top sellers, and to indicate which species they are mainly intended for. This is what they had to say:

SENSAS

Magic: Roach and bream, slow or stillwaters
Magic and Tonic: Skimmer bream, stillwaters
3000: An all-round river mix
2000: Chub, barbel and roach, rivers
Record 515 or 3000 cloud: Cloud bait for rivers

Recommended mixes:
1 x Magic 1 x Tonic 1 x Record 515: Skimmers in slow-moving water.
1 x 300 1 x green or golden bottom mix: Heavy flow mix
1 x 200 $\frac{1}{2}$ x Crusher Hemp or Cupra Molasses: Normal rivers
1 x Z72 Red 1 x 200: Good Trent mix for chub.

VAN DEN EYNDE

Expo Red: Tench, carp and bream, stillwaters
Super Cup: Roach, perch, rudd and bream, canals and lakes
Special Concours: Very fine cloud bait
Kastar: Semi-buoyant, good for heavily silted or weeded waters
(do not over-wet when mixing)

Recommended mixes:
2 x Viva 1 x Expo 1 x Special: Shallow water
2 x Expo 1 x Secret: Deep water
1 x Super Cup 1 x Special: Canals
1 x Super Cup $\frac{1}{2}$ x Brasen: Skimmer mix
$\frac{1}{2}$ x Special 2 x Kastar: Cloud bait
1 x Kastar 1 x Super Cup 1 x Special: For use with a lot of maggots

BRITISH GROUNDBAITS

Catch: Roach, chub, rudd and bream (with Hemp Herbi Attractor)
Meatimix: Carp, tench, barbel and chub (protein mix)
Kestrel (four colours): Multi-purpose, fine cloud
Contest: Special bream attractor.

USEFUL ACCESSORIES

by Tom Pickering

The number of useful accessories now available to the pole angler really underlines the popularity of the method. If it was the minority pastime many still think it is we would not be catered for quite so well. So here's a quick guide to some of the bits and pieces we could not do without.

Top of my list is the Diamond Eye Easy Threader (see picture overleaf), a simple length of springy wire used for threading elastic into the tip sections of poles. The clever bit is the diamond shaped eye. Put the elastic through the eye and pull it into the corner, and it traps tight while being pulled through the pole tip. Carry around a few spare lengths of elastic, ready tied to Stonfos, and it takes but a few seconds to replace a worn or broken elastic on the bank.

The external PTFE bushes, which we once had to make ourselves, now come in packets, and so does the newer internal version. Once a pole tip has been cut back to the right diameter for whichever type of bush you choose to use you can carry spares – preferably ready placed on the spare elastics. Make the latter a little over-length with a loop on the end. Hitch a rubber band into the hook on the Stonfo and you can then carry your spares safely on a pole winder, or one of the frames the elastics are originally sold on.

Pole winders (pictured overleaf) come in a variety of sizes, and must always be longer than the float on the tackle they are storing. For the beginner I should describe how to use a winder. If you are storing a tackle with a hook on it, the hook should go over the thin crosspiece on the winder. If, as I do, you store tackles without the hook, the loop at the hook end of the tackle has to go over the little peg at the end of the winder.

When you have wound the tackle on, the loop at the other end has to attach to one of the pegs on the end of the winder. Where once we had to mess around with rubber bands we now have elasticised pole winder anchors (pictured overleaf). The anchor-shaped end snugs into the loop, and then you just stretch the anchor round to the most suitable peg and loop it on.

If the elastic gets slack in use, or you want to tighten it up to assist better hooking, or to persuade fish to come out a bit faster, the Elastic Tensioner (also pictured overleaf) offers a rapid way of doing it. It's a plastic device with a hook at either end. One hook goes into the loop at the end of the Uni-Bung. Then you

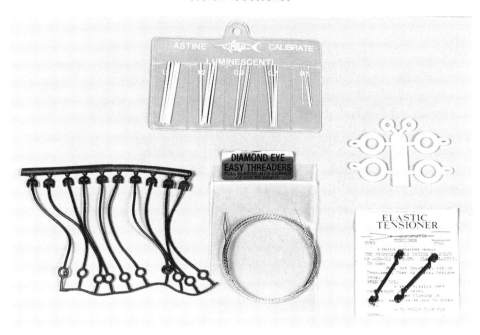

Small but essential accessories. At the top, different colours and thicknesses of interchangeable pole float bristles. To the left, pole winder anchors. Centre, the Diamond Eye Threader, without which re-rigging with elastic can be a very difficult job. Right (top) are Hook-up rings, which act either as hook carriers or depth markers when rolled on to the pole. Below them are Elastic Tensioners, which offer a rapid way of tightening up slack elastic.

"shorten" the elastic by taking it a few times round the tensioner as shown on the manufacturer's diagram. Simple, but clever!

The Uni-Bung itself, the rear end attachment for internal elastic systems, was mentioned in the Flicktips and Elastic Systems chapter, but here's a picture (opposite page) as it emerges from the packet. It has to be cut down to less than half its length for carbon poles, but it is also made to be used with glass poles, which are wider in their internal diameter. Another simple, cheap and clever device.

Empty pole tackle winders.

Close-up of the Uni-Bung, currently the best back-end for the internal elastic system. Its use was explained in the "Flicktips and Elastic Systems" chapter.

An old back step on a sloping concrete drive, but it serves to illustrate how effective this adjustable leg system is for uneven terrain. It also comes with a set of longer legs for standing in water.

Another invaluable bolt-on accessory is an instantly adjustable pole-holder. This type is one of the best available.

In the text of this book I have mentioned only the Streamline tungsten olivettes, but there are also lead free olivettes on the market which are very good. One special merit is that they are colour coded, so you can see at a glance what size it is. They do them in .20, .30, .50, .70, 1.00, 1.35 and 1.50 gramme sizes.

Interchangeable tips, for the floats designed to take them, are invaluable to give us instant colour changes, though do remember the little dodge I mentioned elsewhere about dipping new tips into Mucilin grease. It keeps the float waterproof.

Hook-up rings (pictured on page 136) are cheap – and priceless. When a pole is rigged up, but not being used, these rubberised rings can be rolled to the appropriate place on the pole. The hook is then latched into the little tab, which prevents it catching something it shouldn't. A secondary use for these rings, and the sole use for the smaller ones without tabs, is as depth markers, after a swim has been plumbed.

Bolt-on accessories for tackle boxes are now a boom industry. Our boxes can now be turned into secure and level platforms via adjustable legs, with a variety of slot-on accessories which make you feel a bit like a Dalek. But they are well-designed and efficient, nowadays. I will leave the reader to research that market himself, but the system pictured on page 137 takes some beating.

One bolt-on device which is a real must is an adjustable pole holder. I have pictured (on page 138) the one I think is currently the best available. The front and rear hooks are instantly adjustable, and capable of holding any length of pole clear of the water when you need both hands for some other job.

Pole technology is advancing so fast there will undoubtedly be some other vital accessory on the market by the time we get into print. But if you have read this book from cover to here you are bang up to date with the development of the method, and the simple and advanced ways in which the pole is used.

Mastery of the method is now up to you, but hopefully you will draw some inspiration from the remaining sections of the book. Some great names in pole fishing, and the names of every angler who has represented England at European and World Championship level, are mentioned in our history of the World Championship – the competition which gave birth to pole fishing as we know it today.

Almost everything we know about the pole sprang from this event, and winning it became the Holy Grail of match fishing. I was privileged to be in the team when we finally made it, but until Colin Dyson's patient research began to bring the whole story together I did not appreciate the full implications of what we had done.

WORLD CHAMPIONSHIP HISTORY 1957-1983

THE DIFFICULT YEARS

by Colin Dyson

The precise moment when British anglers began to take pole fishing seriously is hard to isolate, but it was inevitably bound up with the World Championships. For many years this event did not seem to be considered of much importance by our anglers or administrators - strange though that may seem in the light of attitudes which now prevail. If they really did care, they had a funny way of showing it.

Our involvement in international competition began in 1951, with a match on the Thames, organised to celebrate the Festival of Britain. It was fished by teams from France, Belgium, Holland, Denmark, the US forces based in Britain and 45 associations affiliated to the National Federation of Anglers. Birmingham won it, incidentally, with Coventry second, and we dominated the individual result as well. The continentals struggled. We were to pay for it later!

Whether that Festival event was directly responsible for the foundation of the Confederation Internationale de la Peche Sportive (CIPS) is something I have been unable to discover. What is certain, though, is that an international conference involving the governing bodies of angling in many different countries was held in Rome in February, 1952. Our National Federation of Anglers sent delegates, and CIPS was formed in some style. The Italian Federation's hospitality even included a private audience with the Pope!

There were lofty ideals behind the formation of CIPS, few of which have come to anything. Organising competitions seems to have been the main surviving achievement, and they wasted no time. They ran what was first called a European Championship, on Italy's Lake Garda in 1953. The Leeds and Birmingham teams, first and second in the 1952 National Championship on the River Severn, provided five men apiece, more or less at the last moment, and they beat France and Italy. We had the admirable Kenny Kendall, from Leeds, in third individual place.

Kenny, still going strong at 72, remembers this match as unique. It was the only match in which he finished both first and third! "There was some sort of fiddle on," he says. "The rules got changed overnight, and although I finished up with top weight the organisers gave me the third place medal. As far as the NFA were concerned I'd won, so I later got a winning medal from them." Kenny drily observes that they won the team event under both sets of rules!

The NFA, despite their help in the foundation of CIPS, were lukewarm about the new event at this stage. In 1954 they refused to send a team to the European Championship in Germany, and urged member associations to have nothing to do with the match. Their main worry was a rule that catches should be killed, but there had also been rumblings of discontent about the way the '53 team had been selected, and concern about the cost. Coventry, however, ignored the NFA's recommendations, and put together a Midlands team to fish for England. They won again, and official attitudes changed to such an extent that the NFA offered to run the third European Championship on the Thames at Reading. This was probably the match which set the scene for many years of failure. Instead of picking a team of Thames experts the fatal decision was made to allow the top five teams in the National Championship to nominate one angler. Democratic, maybe, but disastrous. England finished fifth on a river badly out of sorts.

In 1956, on the River Seine in Paris, the same selection system sent six anglers - one from each of the top six teams in the famous Huntspill National. According to my research the lads took this one really seriously. Their preparation included visits to the Moulin Rouge and the Casino de Paris! But why not? The team had paid half the £40 cost themselves, and the match itself was an utter fiasco. One of our anglers, Gerry Woodcock, claims the swims were six feet long, the water 12 to 14ft deep and the banks "20ft high" - a probable exaggeration, but it is easy to picture their predicament. Anyway, they fished as though they were still seeing spinning roulette wheels and high kicking dancing girls, finishing last of seven!

Even six years later the approach had not changed much. George Robinson (Newark) mostly remembers the 1962 match on Lake Garda for the fact that the team wound up totally penniless by the time they got there. Bernard Donovan (who became manager three years later) wired home for assistance, and was sent £100 by Coventry & District AA, who might not have approved of the way some of it was spent! It purchased a certain produce of Bonny Scotland, and since talking to George I have had to change my mental image of former NFA President, the late Major Brian Halliday. He came across in later years as a bit of a stuffed shirt, but genuine members of that club surely do not frolic on street corners, flogging old newspapers to passers-by!

Scratch the surface of any match in this era, and money (or the lack of it) comes to the fore. When Ken Horton thought he had qualified as Coventry's top weight National man for the world event in Luxembourg in 1963 he had to borrow £2 to buy his passport. He went on to find that Coventry had nominated Billy Lane instead, apparently because Billy's father had offered to meet the cost! Ken, who never did get abroad on that passport, wonders to this day what he might have done off Billy's peg. Some regarded him as a better angler, then, than Billy, who grabbed the chance to become our first world champion and, of course, the first real super star matchman of the modern era.

The only known picture of Billy Lane, from Coventry, winning the World Championship individual title in Luxembourg in 1963. He was the first of England's World champions

CIPS had decided to upgrade their event to World Championship status in 1957, but the NFA made an inglorious start. After hunting long and hard for the names of those who fished for us at Smederevo, Yugoslavia, I eventually I discovered they had not even sent a team. They cited "distance reasons," according to one report I unearthed, though I imagine that cost was the real consideration. Funds were short, and not all the member clubs were wholeheartedly behind these jaunts into Europe.

Happily we have taken part in every world match since 1957, but apart from modest third places in East Germany in 1961 and Yugoslavia in 1967 our teams achieved no more than we could have expected throughout the 1950s and 1960s, a period brightened only by two individual victories. Robin Harris followed up Billy Lane's Luxembourg triumph with a win in West Germany in 1969.

Lane's formidable presence in the team, as we now know, owed nothing to shrewd selection (except possibly on the part of the Coventry association). The managers, Tom Draper (up to 1965), Bernard Donovan (1966 to 1970) and also Stan Smith, in his first year in charge, were all stuck with one man from each of the leading National Championship teams. Almost invariably these teams nominated their top catchers, some of whom had amassed bream weights with methods which were not even allowed in the World Championships!

The system sometimes ensured that some very capable individuals represented their country. Many of the most famous names in match fishing, twenty or more years ago, marched into the fray. It will be easy for the match man of today, however, to imagine how unsuitable were many of the actual teams we sent. World Championship rules have changed many times, but one constant factor has been the method of deciding the team championship –

points scored by each angler. For the first few years they added together the overall placings of each man to get the team total. Later they changed to the section points system, but either way just one weak link was potentially terminal, and our selection method virtually ensured at least one.

Rarely did we send a team which had even half a chance, for even when the haphazard selection system managed to throw up a competent looking team one rather large obstacle remained. While they were fishing the same venues at the same times as the continentals, our randomly selected internationals were only just participating in the same sport! The rules were framed for pole fishing, a method not then employed here. The restriction to the use of not more than 15 metres of line, which was often in force, was not a fiendish plot to handicap our teams. It was a logical limit in an event in which swims were short, by our standards, and there were dire penalties for anyone who allowed a float to stray out of the allotted area. Many of our teams had to live with that handicap and a variety of other apparently strange rules.

One rule - the five minute period for heavy baiting - was geared to their method of fishing the bloodworm. Nowadays we all understand what they were doing with those amazingly heavy bombardments, but it was years before any of our internationals realised what it was

Robin Harris from Peterborough, World Champion in West Germany in 1969.

all about - partly because most of our early representatives only ever fished the one time. In the final analysis the lack of continuity was the ultimate weakness of our selection policy.

The more one thinks about the set-up the more absurd it becomes. We could not send pole anglers to a match perpetually won on the pole, simply because we did not have any. Neither could we send bloodworm anglers to a match almost invariably won on the bloodworm because our system was virtually programmed not to select them! Not many of our Nationals, then, were on waters where bloodworm men were likely to shine.

They were wasted and misleading years; years which fostered myths and misunderstanding. It was the widespread belief, for example, that it was only the silly rules which prevented us from showing the rest of the world how superior our methods were. The pole, we were told, would slide into oblivion in an even contest against rod and reel.

The first top class international to tumble to the pole's potential was Kevin Ashurst, when the selection system produced him for duty in Holland in 1970. In fact it was his father Benny who had qualified, but he stepped down in Kevin's favour. It was a gesture which had far-reaching effects on our match scene. Even though Kevin was out of his depth that day his brain was working perfectly. He noted the way the continentals handled their poles, the precision the system gave them in bait presentation, how bites were emphasised by delicate floats and how easily those bites were effectively struck with gentle lifts of the pole.

Kevin came and went without attracting any attention whatever from the all-conquering continentals. Years later, however, they were to recognise him as the finest all-round angler in the game. He was to become a top performer at world level among those currently operating, and behind three-times world champion Robert Tesse and very few others in overall World Championship achievement. But all that was in the future when Kevin crept home from Holland, chastened, but carrying the burning resolve to master the pole. He soon became one of the leaders of the coming revolution in English pole fishing.

That, and the triumphs of Lane and Harris, were the only significant moments for England from 1957 to 1971, when Stan Smith took over as manager following the sudden death of Bernard Donovan. We soon realised we had a vastly different character in charge; a man determined to change England's fortunes. Unfortunately he made a bad start, and he and I fell out over a matter not worth repeating this far on, but it soured our relationship for years afterwards. I tried to make allowances for the fact that his opening match in Italy was, after all, a first attempt, and that he had not had very much time to prepare for it. He was saddled with anglers who had

Stan Smith from Coleshill, England Manager from 1971-1983.

no known form for the type of water they were fishing, and it may have been the certainty of defeat which both affected his planning and caused him to build a protective wall around himself. He became a taciturn, difficult man with no time at all for the angling Press. It remains a matter for argument whether this was the result of Press criticism or the cause of it, but he certainly got far worse publicity than he really deserved.

He got off on the wrong foot in the publicity stakes - a situation he never remedied - but he did not get much credit for one side of the job which he did particularly well. He could put himself about politically, within the National Federation of Anglers and at the often stormy meetings of CIPS. He was a tough negotiator with two vital aims, both of which were to ensure future successes for the England team. One was to campaign at CIPS for the abolition of line limits, which he got in the end. The other fundamental achievement was to persuade the NFA to make the manager the sole selector. He won that battle in time for the 1972 match in Czechoslovakia, and it is only from then on that it is really valid to assess the reign of Stan Smith as manager of England.

The immortal quote from Dick Clegg, when he took over from Smith in 1984, was that he had been guilty of nothing except being unlucky. I mostly go along with that. Stan's luck was bad from the start. The 1972 match, on a pacey river full of fish, was fished under the 15 metre line limit rule. There is no doubt in the minds of anyone who was out there that England would have walked it with unrestricted line. We were second, with 24 points, 12 behind France. It was our best result to date, but without a line limit Smith would almost certainly have triumphed with the first team he had personally selected.

Next year, at Chalons-sur-Soane, in France, Smith had unlimited line to work with on a water which responded to bloodworm at close range! It was perfect for the French and Belgians, but England were third, earning praise from Robert Tesse, then manager of the French team. He was a cunning and perceptive man, and perhaps saw what was coming. They had known, he said, what individuals like Billy Lane could do, but they had never considered England a threat as a team. "Now we know different," he said.

But 17 years of pole domination had remained intact, and in the 1974 match at Ghent, in Belgium, Smith made our very first brave attempt to win with the pole. Not only that, he took them on with bloodworm too. This was real desperation stuff, but nothing else was working. We finished a fairly creditable sixth, but there were rumbles at home about the team he had picked. It certainly wasn't the best we could have fielded for a bloodworm match, though we have to remember that Smith never had the resources now available to Clegg for the in-depth study of venues. Often the right approach was learned only when the teams were over there for their one and only practice run.

Ian Heaps became our third individual champion in Poland in 1975, another year in which it would have been a total waste of time for Smith to fill in pools coupons. Half an hour from the end Tesse had written off France and even congratulated his English rival on his first team success. We had Heaps and Ashurst winning sections, Ivan Marks and Tony Scott well-placed and, even though Terry Payne was in dire trouble France had two in the same boat. Tesse's congratulations were premature. One of his strugglers, Etienne Guibert, suddenly started to catch, and went soaring up from about last to third in Ashurst's section.

That left the dejected Terry Payne, 16th and last in section with one little roach and a foulhooked stickleback, to take the rap for a three point defeat. Manfully, he accepted the responsibility, but the angling world over here have either forgotten or never knew that the great French angler Guy Hebert also scored 16 points in a similarly duff peg. It puts Payne's plight into perspective, but to this day he can't forget that a mere $3\frac{1}{2}$oz more from him would have given England their long-awaited victory.

Ian Heaps from Stockport became our third individual champion in Poland in 1975.

In these last few matches the pole was part of the English armoury, but in 1976, in Bulgaria, they were to see this weapon in a totally different perspective. It was a match the Bulgarians apparently tried to fiddle for their own team. Managers able to get there to practice were taken to one not very productive end of the vast reservoir, Lake Georgi Traikov. The immediate pre-match practice was there, too, and it was only the voluble insistence of France and Italy in particular which finally persuaded the Bulgars to permit a brief glimpse of the actual match length the evening before.

They took us to a great dam wall. The Italians looked over it and did a few cartwheels. It was heaving with bleak - dense black shoals of them - but here and there we could see rather bigger fish below them, mostly little chub. We had heard the Italians were good on bleak, and to judge from the way they were jumping around with big smiles on their faces the rest were fishing for second. So it proved. Even having seen it I find it difficult to describe how good they were with short poles and surface fishing, so I'll leave it to the statistics.

Fausto Passinetti took 615 bleak weighing about 27lbs in three hours, and with two other section wins with similar catches, and two second places, Italy walked it. For quite some time, though, Stan Smith was clearly under the impression that England were winning. Ken Giles was later highly critical about the quality of the information he and the rest received during the match. To finish 11th in section after thinking he was leading it, or thereabouts, must have been devastating, though to be fair it was a very tricky match to keep track of. England were catching fewer but bigger fish, but one could not look anywhere without seeing fish flying through the air. I hadn't a clue where we stood.

Ken Giles from Birmingham.
He was critical of the quality of
information received by the
England team during the famous
bleak match in Bulgaria in 1976.

Smith had no way of finding out in advance what this match was going to be like, but as the weigh-in became a marathon (fish had to be weighed and counted, for there were points for every fish and for each gramme of weight to work out) his team had the chance to consider tactics for the individual match to follow. This was the first event in which the individual title was to be settled in a separate match, and Ivan Marks and Kevin Ashurst had finished high enough in their sections to qualify for it.

Having seen what the Italians could do off the top they elected to pole fish with heavier gear to get through to the bigger fish. It had taken so long to sort out the first result, though, that only 90 minutes could be allowed for the new style individual event. Any longer than that and they would have been counting and weighing in the dark!

The scene was set for a fascinating encounter. The Italians had also learned during the first match, and they stepped up a gear. Dino Bassi went on to win his second title with 384 fish weighing about 17lbs in 90 minutes! To put that in perspective the all-time record for the championship was, and still is, 652 fish in 180 minutes by the Belgian Isenbaert in Yugoslavia in 1967. Bassi was on course for over 750 in that time.

Marks was second with 190 better fish weighing 7.985 kilos, only 284 grammes (about 10oz) short of Bassi. Passinetti took third, with a luckless Ashurst mere fractions behind in fourth. He lost the title because of a tangled tackle on his flicktip pole rig inside the last half hour. After taking a short time trying to sort it out he had to pick up a pole rigged with elastic, and get it adjusted right, for the last 20 minutes. It neither struck fish properly nor lifted them as quickly, and he lost by 1lb 3$\frac{1}{2}$oz. Imagine that weight separating the top four in a match of that quality. OK, Kevin should have had duplicate rigs made up, but there had barely been time to set up two short poles between draw time and the start.

This trip was also memorable for my second major brush with the manager. It blew up after he had brusquely refused to hand over his and his team's passports to the Bulgarian who asked for them at the hotel in Varna. He was left in no doubt that British passports were British property, and no way were they to be left in communist hands! I thought a query as to why he might want them was in order, so when the chap stalked off I followed him and put the question. "Because," he answered, "I cannot make the arrangements for your return flight to England without them."

Stan Smith had made the arrangements for the whole party, which included the journalists and the VIPs, NFA President Fred Jennings and Trevor Beaumont, from Shakespeare, who were sponsors at that time. I figured there was a good enough reason to hand over my passport. I collected others from journalists and from the team, and handed them in. When Stan found out he was not at all pleased, nor was he impressed with the explanation. He had made the travel arrangements, and it was all sorted out. Would I please stop interfering...? I did. Nobody got around to collecting the passports of Fred

Jennings and Trevor Beaumont, who had split off from the party to stay at another hotel. When the names were called for the flight home from Sofia everyone got on the plane except one very angry NFA President and one extremely unhappy sponsor!

Smith, who survived much longer than the sponsorship deal, made one change for Luxembourg in 1977, leaving out Ken Giles, who was not surprised. Dickie Carr was called up for Smith's second attempt to win with pole and bloodworm. Ian Heaps won his section, finishing 16th in the individual match, the team came fifth and they all got home OK.

Criticism was mounting at home about team selection and tactics. Ken Giles and his great friend Clive Smith, the Birmingham skipper many thought should succeed his namesake, were particularly severe, but nothing rattled the England boss. In 1978 he boldly selected Tom Pickering for the first time, and Mark Downes got in too, after a spell as reserve. Marks, Ashurst and Heaps completed the line-up for a match on a massive canal. England, with unlimited line (the limit had been dropped, thanks to Stan Smith, after the 1974 match) were the clear favourites to win. They dominated the practice sessions with sliding floats.

There wasn't a team which did not think that England would win, so how come they finished last, their worst world match placing ever, under any selection system? It was down to Stan Smith's jinx again. England had been the only team catching in near perfect conditions, with cloud cover and a big wind which really got the water moving. The pole and bloodworm brigade were in serious trouble - until match day dawned. The wind had blown itself out. Not a breath. The sky had cleared in the night, and, as I put it at the time in a report for Angler's Mail, "the sun blazed pitilessly down and the temperature soared into the 80s.."

England had no back-up plan. They had gone for broke, and broke they were. Heaps was fishless, and last in section, a placing duplicated by Downes, with three fish, and Pickering with two. Ashurst was 16th and Marks 11th. It was simply unbelievable, and much as I disliked Stan Smith by then I was desperately sorry for him. "I know what they'll be saying back home," he said, "but I'd do it exactly the same way tomorrow." Obviously we had nobody in the individual match, an event nobody watched more intently than Tom Pickering. It is interesting to note, here, just how quick in the brain Tommy was over a decade ago. After watching a peg to peg battle for the title between Jean Pierre Fougeat (France) and the Italian Roberto Trabucco this is Tom's assessment of Trabucco's downfall. I have kept it all these years, certain it would come in useful some time.

"It was a terrible mistake which cost Trabucco the title," he said. "He was hammering Fougeat with bleak, but he went to pieces when Fougeat caught two fish, a roach and a nase of about 8oz apiece from the 10 metre line. Trabucco suddenly panicked, and put down the short pole. He was obviously wondering if there were good fish on his own 10 metre mark, but as soon as he picked up

Austria 1978… England finished last of 18 in a match they could have won.

his longer pole Fougeat knifed him. It was brilliant. He piled feed into the short line and took Trabucco's bleak away. When he didn't catch out he came inside, and couldn't catch there either. If he hadn't got upset he would have won. He needed only five more bleak, which he would certainly have got. But what an angler Fougeat was, to spot that opening so quickly. These men aren't just superb pole anglers; they are brilliant tacticians. I wish I could watch them for a year, but in $2^{1}/_{2}$ hours I learned so much…"

Fougeat, who had taken the killing fish, a 2lb bream, minutes after Trabucco dropped his clanger, won with 11 fish weighing 1550 grammes - 1561 points. Trabucco had 96 fish for 1400g and 1496 points.

I realised then what England had been up against all those years, and marvelled at Pickering's resilience. He just shrugged off that last in section, took the chance to watch the world's top pole men - and went home to find a night school class in French!

Pickering's friend and mentor Denis White got the call for a tough canal match in Spain in 1979. France won again, with England 7th, White and Ashurst making the individual match and finishing 23rd and 31st respectively. By now the only match anglers not criticising aspects of selection were those Smith was picking. It was quite a surprise when one of his critics, Clive Smith, was called into the squad for the match on Germany's River Neckar in 1980, but he ended up reserve.

Germany had picked this one for their own team, and they obliged with four section wins and a third. With 7 points they were well clear of England, second with 23. No hard luck story this time; Germany simply knew too much about their own water. They got the top two places in the individual match, with Ashurst 6th, Clive Smith 10th, Marks 12th and Tony Scott 16th. Pickering, fishing for the second time, did not qualify and neither did Heaps.

The impact of the 1981 disaster when England were expected to walk it on their own territory, the Warwickshire Avon at Luddington, might well have registered on the Richter Scale as a small earthquake. So might some of the pre-match controversy! Everybody could name a venue before it was finally announced; nobody had suggested Luddington. Everybody could pick a team to win at Luddington; perm any five from about 200. It was a piece of cake. Cruelty to continentals was added to Stan's list of "crimes."

The NFA really went to town on this match. They even got the backing of the Midland Bank, so no expense was spared. The angling media's enthusiasm knew no bounds, but Stan Smith rarely seemed ready to release information when they wanted it. Angling Times took him apart for it, pointing out quite rightly that it wasn't fair to the sponsor to organise the great match in secret. It all bounced off the rhino hide of the manager, though in different circumstances even he might have smiled when a long stream of accusations about inefficiency and other shortcomings culminated in the escape of Angling Times' advertising balloon from the headquarters site. It fouled with power lines, depriving part of Warwickshire of its electricity supply!

Although Stan Smith did not sneak out in the dead of night to cut it free it was undoubtedly his fault. His famous hoodoo had struck yet again! That balloon was torn loose by the overnight storm which turned the HQ site into a quagmire and the Avon into a raging torrent. Our team of Clive Smith, Tony Scott, Dave Thomas, Kevin Ashurst and John Dean, who were supposed merely to turn up and collect their gold medals, went home with silver instead. Again we had no back-up plan, and the French proved better at winkling out priceless points with their trusty poles and deadly

Dave Thomas from Leeds whose individual victory was the sole consolation for England after the disaster on the Warwickshire Avon.

bloodworms. We had to take what little comfort we could from a fine individual win by Dave Thomas, who also won his section in the team match.

That consolation apart it was a tragedy for all concerned, but for Smith most of all. More than a decade of dreams had gone into that match, and he had surely earned one moment of glory. Bearing in mind all the difficulties previously outlined I do not think his record was at all bad. There were so many near misses, and two victories, possibly three, were taken from him almost by divine intervention. He was clearly not a man to cross a busy road with, that's for sure! Short of those I have known who have been struck down by accidents and fatal illnesses I have never known an unluckier man.

Luddington was the beginning of the end for Stan, but it takes time to remove an institution. He stayed on for two more matches, both of which we were virtual carbon copies of what had gone on before. On Ulster's Newry Canal in 1982 England finished third, six points behind Holland and one behind France. We had lost another Championship we were favourites to win, though this match was a milestone for Kevin Ashurst. Smith saw his favourite matchman take top weight in the team match - enough at one time to have made him champion. Sadly, on a canal which was out of sorts, the others could not back him. They returned three scores of 6 and a 7.

It was the individual match which made this a memorable occasion. Big Kev figured what he could do once he could do again, and in a tremendous late burst he came through to win the title. Just 12 years after he had first seen the method, he had become the first Englishman to win the world crown on the pole! Until then nobody could have convinced me it could be exciting to watch someone catching a mere 1lb 10oz of bits. But the match had been almost anybody's as the time ticked away, and when Kevin's legendary patience began to pay off the atmosphere was electric. The last two or three bites seemed to be induced by the sheer willpower of the watching crowd. Nobody more deserved to win the ultimate crown.

If we are to seek a hard luck story in Smith's final match, on the Rhine Canal in Holland in 1983, then it has to lie in the scores. England, hand-picked to take on the continentals with the pole on an excellent fishery, fished bloodworm, pinkie and caster to return their best ever points score of 14. They beat the host country by 10 clear points, but lost by 5. Belgium, a fading force in the previous few years, knew the canal as well as the Dutch, and they were just too good on the day. Six times in the decade that England score would have been enough. Alan McAtee and Ian Heaps won their sections. Kevin Ashurst was second, Dave Roper fourth and Dickie Carr sixth.

If Stan Smith ever sits down and studies his record he will probably conclude that this was his best result. He had seen England, starting from scratch, achieve virtual parity with the best at pole fishing. In the 12 years he picked the team they were second five times and third twice. He had battled to change the rules to create a fair contest between the pole and rod and reel. He had blooded a sizable squad of anglers, most of whom could stand the heat of battle at top

The great breakthrough... Kevin Ashurst from Leigh (Lancs.) became the first Englishman to win the World title on the pole, on the Newry Canal in Northern Ireland in 1982.

Big smile for the small catch which gave Ashurst the title on the Newry Canal.

level. He turned an international joke into one of the most feared teams in the world.

Is this really what is known as failure? I really don't think so. The task, when he first faced it, was monumental. Anybody taking it on would have had to learn, probably by their mistakes. They would have had to wait, too, for the talent they could call on to mature. Instant success wasn't on the cards for anybody.

Dick Clegg did not inherit a sinking ship, by any means. England had come in 2,2,3,2 in their last four matches, and on their last outing they had beaten every top pole nation in the world, bar one, at their own game. Could the continentals have foreseen that in 1972? I doubt it, but they were probably not at all surprised at what was to come under Dick Clegg, who was smart enough to choose virtually all his men from Smith's battle-hardened list. I will leave Tom Pickering to summarise Clegg's reign to date, for he was in the thick of it. He can tell most of it from the inside.

Two of the legendary figures in World Championship history – Billy Lane (left), and the only man to win the individual crown three times, Robert Tesse (France).

WORLD CHAMPIONSHIP HISTORY 1984-1988

THE TRIUMPHANT YEARS

by Tom Pickering

I have to admit to being in two minds when Dick Clegg got the England manager's job, following the removal of Stan Smith after the 1983 match. I knew he could do some of it well, having seen the results of his efforts with the Barnsley side. He was tough, ruthless when he had to be, shrewd on the tactical side and could generate loyalty among those he had fishing for him. Had he not become England manager he had a match angling record easily good enough to make him a contender for a place in the England team. He was therefore well-qualified to judge the abilities of others. Another vital qualification was that was was not notably unlucky at anything to do with match fishing, and especially in the major events.

So why was I in two minds? Partly because I thought he was too much of an angler. I wondered whether he could perform at meetings of the NFA and CIPS as effectively as Stan Smith did, and whether he could organise the vital matters not directly concerning the team and tactics. I can remember thinking he would be a terrific coach, for that was the area where Stan Smith had needed some help. The two of them together, I felt, would have been a formidable combination. It was not long, however, before I realised I had underestimated Dick in those areas I was unsure about. He hasn't put a foot wrong anywhere, and where his strengths were obvious he has really excelled.

I am a great believer in team atmosphere, for when that's right you get the best results. I think his biggest success has been to get his squads working together as one determined unit. Where some of Stan's teams split into two, in effect, his have been 100 per cent loyal to him and to each other, holding nothing back. We have seen that especially well in the attitudes of those unfortunate to become reserves. Alan McAtee has performed in that role three times, giving tremendous support to those who fished. Dave Roper, Bob Nudd and Dave Vincent have done the same, and it's a vital job - every bit as important as actually fishing. It must be an awful moment for the one not chosen, and the manager, when the time comes, but it must be easier to accept when you know the manager has always been there supervising the practice sessions, watching and weighing up what is required. When the team is fishing Dick is always there.

One big worry I had when Dick got the job was the knowledge of how tough it would be for him to select members of his own team, including Denis White and me, of course. It would have been easier for him to prove his impartiality by looking elsewhere, and he must have known perfectly well that if he selected us and failed the knives would be out for him in various quarters. In my view it took a lot of guts to select us for his first team for the River Thielle in Switzerland, along with Kevin Ashurst, Ian Heaps, Bob Nudd and Alan McAtee.

It's history what happened now. We tied on points with Luxembourg, England's best ever placing, and the main reason for Dick not gaining outright victory at the first attempt was my 11 point score. Just one point less from me, and it would not have gone to that sad defeat on weight. I was heartbroken, but tried hard not to let it show.

Back home the result was regarded as a success, blighted by bad luck. Luxembourg had a better draw with some end pegs, and they caught the bonus chub which eluded us. We weren't griping, though. It's all part of match fishing, and we were later to see the other side of that particular coin. I was now certain we would win that long-awaited title fairly soon, though. There was something in the Swiss air, almost, which told me so. The organisation had been good, and the tactics sound. Above all there was a confidence about the lads in the squad which sprang both from past experience at this level and from the way we were led. There was no feeling that Dick had inherited Stan Smith's jinx. Instead we saw it as the big breakthrough, for we had outscored all the really noted teams.

My only doubt was whether I would be there when the great breakthrough finally came. Whatever the reasons for it I had not exactly made myself an automatic choice for the Arno, in Italy, in 1985, and was very relieved to get the call. Dick hadn't blamed me, obviously, and he went on to field exactly the same team. The spirit of Switzerland was still there, too, and I began to feel we were on a winner as soon as we got to Italy - 12 days before the match. This was thanks to the continued sponsorship of H. Steade & Sons Ltd, who had come in to back us the year before. Their money had made an impact in Switzerland, but it was even more valuable in Italy. We had seen the Arno the previous year, and were now there in force, with plenty of time to get a plan worked out.

Dick simply told us to get on with practice, at first, and to get rid of our preconceptions. "Then we'll get our heads together, and sort out what's right and what's wrong," he said. What emerged was that it was possible to catch 4 to 5ft deep on the waggler in water generally a lot deeper. We learned that sections A and B were full of fish, and therefore we should do OK. The shallow E section was a straightforward waggler job which would present no problems either. It was the deep C and D sections

England manager Dick Clegg: "Sort out what's right", he said.

which we were a bit concerned about. They didn't hold as many fish, but they did have lots of small, lethally spined catfish. First we had to learn how to catch them without damaging ourselves, but the big bonus was the discovery that redworm caught the bigger catfish. It worked every time we slipped one on in practice, though we had to take care that Italian eyes were not watching at the time.

The match plan was simple. It was to be shallow waggler in all sections at the start, then twelve metre pole or slider in C and D when results dictated a change. Bob Nudd drew A with me in B, but for some reason there was a separate draw in these two sections. I drew next to the Italian, Gabba, and in the other three sections the other lads had drawn next to Italy which is exactly what we wanted. We wanted to pressurise them; to let them know we were there. The last thing we had wanted was to have them between two less rated teams fishing nice and relaxed and with us out of sight and out of mind. Having got what we wanted, we were subjected to some tremendous pressure from the crowd. For some reason it not only did not bother me, it fired me up instead. I'd seen a swim full of small chub up top, and realised that now was the time to justify the faith two managers had shown in me. If I didn't win that section, I told myself, I would never win one.

The feeling as the start approached was really strange. I was totally at ease, and full of confidence. I hadn't had a good result for England, but this time I just knew it would be different – and it was. I piled groundbait and loose feed onto the 12 metre line to keep my fish from straying to Gabba, and sprayed loose feed as far out as I could get it with the catapult. The waggler brought me 3lbs of chub in five casts, with Gabba much the same. It was close all through, with me feeling I had the upper hand all the time. His fish were greeted with thunderous applause from a packed crowd. Mine reduced them to total silence, which allowed me to hear encouragement from a small contingent of anglers from Leeds.

There was one spell when I lost the chub, and reserve Dave Roper came along to tell me to pile maggots in even more - three pouches every cast. It worked. I started to catch carrasios, fish like small carp, and the crowd lost its voice completely, except to greet one I lost with tremendous cheering. Clearly it angered Gabba, for as the noise died down again I heard him shouting: "Peekering... take no notice. They are ignorant people..." He must have known he was losing, then, but he had not lost his sense of sportsmanship. I think he also brought the crowd to their senses too, for at the end they gave both of us a great reception.

Only then did I start to feel nervous, for I heard that a Belgian had weighed in 5.8 kilos. I wasn't sure whether I had beaten that, but then I realised that if I had done the Belgian he might do us a favour by pushing Gabba down a place. That's how it worked out, with me on 6.35 and Gabba on 5.5. This was absolutely critical to the overall result, and an indication of how vital a bit of luck can be at this level.

With Denis White winning his section, Ian Heaps and Kevin Ashurst second in theirs, and Bob Nudd having the same sort of grueller I had the year before, we totalled 16 points, with Italy on 17. The luck had finally gone our way, thanks to that intervention by the Belgian. After 28 years of hopeless endeavour, growing professionalism and, eventually, ruthlessly efficient work and planning, England had finally won a world title. To cap it all we were to see our reserve Dave Roper turning in a superb waggler float performance next day, winning the individual crown which I hope to wear one day, should fortune smile. The celebrations were long and uproarious. It was a day none of us will ever forget.

The weigh-in on the River Arno was a nailbiter, but it was the Belgian competitor's catch which proved decisive. He pushed the Italian down a place and gave England their first team victory by a single point.

A glance at the record list might suggest that we were still celebrating the following year at Strasbourg, France, where we plunged to 7th place on a really tough water. It has to be tough when someone like Denis White can score 23 points, but even if he had won his section we would still have been no better than third. The least said about this match the better, perhaps, except to make the point that you can't get it right all the time. The water dropped lower and slower for the match, and fished very different to the practice sessions. I think we fed wrong with jokers and maggot. The Italians, who won, put a lot of pinkies in, and we got done by the Poles at the next peg. They used a tremendous amount of bloodworm, and it seemed to work.

I finished 5th in section and missed the individual match by an ounce. I would have got in if the Frenchman Fougeat had been disqualified for wading in to net a fish, which was against the rules, but he survived an objection. It was a pity from my point of view, for the individual venue was a waggler job. An Austrian was bagging up on it before he lost his bottle when victory beckoned, and Clive Branson took second for Wales on that method. For some reason our two finalists wouldn't change from the pole. Not one of our better weekends, but if the other teams had thought we were in decline they were soon to be disillusioned.

With Stevie Gardener coming in to replace Bob Nudd for the 1987 match on the Mondego River, in Portugal, we were to win with one of the best points scores in the history of the match. We got section wins from Denis and Kevin, second places from Ian Heaps and me, with Stevie turning in a brilliant third in his debut match. Our total of 9 points has been bettered only five times, with the previous year's winners Italy returning 18.

One important point to make at this stage is that while the English anglers had been busily trying to master the pole in the past decade or so some of the continentals had been equally keen to learn how to use waggler floats. They had seen what we could do with them, and knew they had to crack it. The Italians and Belgians, in particular, are now very good with the float, and Stevie Gardener's jaw dropped a bit when he first saw the Italian Trabucco performing with it. "Jeez," he said. "He looks better at it than we are." He wasn't far off the mark, though a certain amount of Italian style and elegance can cover up deficiencies in some of the subtleties. I think that is where we still have the edge, but it isn't much of one now. Denis White, for example, won his section by only 100 grammes from a Belgian. Believe me, it takes a very good angler to get that close to Denis over three hours and on the same method.

Dave Roper (Preston) crowned a great weekend when he became England's sixth individual World Champion.

Good as they now are, though, the team championship scores reveal there is still a crucial difference in class on this method. They might get a few individuals who can give us a race, but getting five together is a different story. It was fairly straightforward for us in Portugal - a simple waggler job with sliding or fixed floats in swims varying in depth up to 14 or 15ft, to catch small barbel on the drop. Practice has shown we could get them going in 10 or 15 minutes, and that they would come into pole range inside the last hour. It went more or less to plan, despite overnight rain which lifted the river a metre and turned it red. It did not alter the fishing. We stuck to our plan to feed four or five balls of Sticky Mag at the start, with a new ball every second cast, while feeding the pole line for later.

Our one worry was A section, which was closest to an area restocked with large numbers of small carp and barbel. These fish had been kept in the stocking area by the bait put in by teams practicing for the match, and they were giving the teams a totally wrong idea of the river's potential. There were 40 to 50lb catches, with 20lbs commonplace, but we knew the match length would be a lot harder. We thought, though, that some of those fish could move into A section during the match, perhaps creating an uneven result. Ideally we needed one of our most experienced men there, but Stevie got stuck with the job. His 3 points were really vital. With 2.5 kilos he was only 300 grammes in front of the ninth man in his section, and it is easy enough to see what might have happened to us if Stevie had come apart in his first international. I was happy enough with my score. I was easily done by a Luxembourg angler who found some small carp on a 4 metre pole, but I knew we weren't really fishing against Luxembourg that day.

Stevie Gardener scored three vital points in Portugal to set up England's second win.

All five England men plus our reserve, Bob Nudd, made the individual match next day, and it proved to be one I will not forget in a hurry. I finished fourth, just 10oz behind Clive Branson, of Wales, and missed enough bites in one spell to have won it. I drew 16, next to Trabucco, doing him with the help of a late burst of fish, but I never had the feeling that I was in the hunt at all. The main action was on pegs 11, 12 and 13, which were occupied by Branson, Denis White and Kevin Ashurst. They were catching before I was, if I can discount one early fish, and even after my late catches I still felt I was at least $1\frac{1}{2}$lbs adrift. I couldn't believe how close it was, though - Branson 2.505, Ashurst 2.499, White 2.200 and me with 2.160. One reasonable fish covered the lot of us, and I could have blown my best chance of winning a world title.

I was devastated until I realised how Kevin and Denis must have felt. Big Kev was just half an ounce off his second world title, and nobody more deserves to be the first Englishman to win two. Denis, too, well-deserved a world title to his name, after a long career as a truly great matchman, so maybe my own

Portugal 1987, and England won for the second time. The celebrating squad was Denis White (left), Stevie Gardener, Tom Pickering, manager Dick Clegg, Kevin Ashurst, Ian Heaps and Bob Nudd (reserve).

disappointment wasn't really justified. None of us really begrudged Branson's victory, though, for Wales put an awful lot of effort into that match, having nothing like the resources we had at our disposal, and the result suggests they got a bad draw in the team event. We had seen them as our most dangerous opposition, along with Italy and Belgium, and it was nice to see them going home with the main consolation prize.

That brings us almost up to date. The great victory of 1988, on the Damme Canal in Belgium, is too recent to cover in great detail, and I wasn't there, of course. Dick Clegg picked a pole and bloodworm squad - Ashurst, Dave Roper, Alan McAtee, Vinnie Smith, Bob Nudd and Dave Vincent, and later added Stevie Gardener as waggler back-up when he suspected that the canal might have been changed by heavy restocking. That was a place I was hoping to fill, and there was a lot of comment that Dick had picked the wrong team, especially when it was revealed that England had tied on points with Italy on the first day, mainly on the waggler.

For this match, though, the rules had been changed. It was a two day team event, with the individual championship going to the angler with the best section points aggregate. Next day England tied again with Italy, this time finding the waggler was not as effective. They did most of the damage with the pole, and it stifled the criticism just as quickly as it had started. All I can say is that the canal was the toughest venue an England team has ever won on, and if Cleggy was wrong he must be hoping to be just as wrong in the future! It was a tremendous nailbiter of a match which put England on a hat-trick chance. They will face that prospect in Bulgaria, just a few months after this book was to be published, and I'm just hoping I will be there to help.

It will be a hard fight to get back in, especially with Stevie Gardener doing so well in Belgium. He won a section and came second in the other, losing the world crown to the formidable Fougeat, the man I so admired when I first saw him in Austria. It is anglers like him, Trabucco, Milo Colombo, Marcel Van den Eynde and other great pole men who remind us of the one major challenge which remains for England - to win one on the pole.

I believe we already have the men with the talent to do it, and that the next few years will see that dream fulfilled. It isn't my dream, incidentally. I really don't care what methods England use to win, just so long as they do! If we don't achieve a pole win in the next few years it will be down to the next generation of pole men who, I hope, will derive at least some of the necessary information and inspiration from this book.

ENGLAND v THE WORLD
THE COMPLETE RECORD

by Colin Dyson

As far as I am aware this is the first attempt to assemble a complete record of the European and World Championship events, including the names of all the anglers who has ever represented England at this level. I found it a fascinating job, not least because it reminded me of internationals I had long forgotton, but it was not an easy exercise. Some of the vital information was tucked away in files left by the late Colin Graham. Some was unearthed from the minutes and reports on file at NFA headquarters. Gaps were then filled by reference to the files of Angling Times, Angler's Mail and earlier publications, notably the Midland Angler and the Fishing Gazette.

When those sources were exhausted I completed the job with the help of that wonderful old angler, artist and historian Frank Oates, from York, with the indomitable Maurice Kausman providing valuable assistance with the christian names of anglers who, with a few notable exceptions, are no longer with us. When I approached Maurice he was 84, and recovering from two serious operations. He was still fishing, he said, but friends were having to lash him to trees to stop him falling into the water! How many of us, I wonder, will remain that keen on fishing in our later years?

It was kind of Frank and Maurice to help, but I am not entirely happy with the project. There was no consistency in the way various reporters down the years had done their jobs. Sometimes they gave the number of fish caught, the weight and the points scored. Sometimes one or more of these details would be missing, and, occasionally, all of them! At times, too, the points score and/or the placings of England was not given. On top of all that the rules for the match and the system for deciding the outcome have changed many times. There is a lack of consistency in the way I have to present the records, but nearly all the information I sought is there, in one form or another. Where appropriate I have inserted explanatory notes about rule changes which affect the interpretation of results.

EUROPEAN CHAMPIONSHIP

1953: LAKE GARDA (ITALY):

Kenny Kendall.

Team: 1 England, 2 France, 3 Italy (scores not known).

Individual: 1 Marrillo (Italy) 105 fish (1,991 points), 2 Cesselin (France) 120 (1,970), 3 Kendall (England) 13 (1,585).

England team: Kenny Kendall, Horace Seed, Freddie Friend, Norman Seal and Henry Pollard (all Leeds), Stan Smith, Alf Wagstaff, Charlie Price, Ollie Bayliss and Norman Haynes (all Birmingham).

1954: LAKE RURSEE (W. GERMANY):

Eric Haynes.

Team: 1 England 50 pts, 2 Belgium 70, 3 Italy 71.

Individual: 1 Vigarani (Italy) 2,647 grammes, 2 Fugazza (Italy) 1,690, 3 Andef (W. Germany) 1,060.

England team: Eric Haynes 570 grammes, Albert Harding 455, Billy Lane 307, Fred Pearson 235, Alf Wagstaff 175.

1955: THAMES AT READING:

Ronnie Lye.

Team: 1 Luxembourg 69, 2 Belgium 71, 3 France 74.

Individual: 1 Mailly (France) 3-14-8 (2,448 points), 2 Dufeys (Belgium) 3-12-14 (2,429), 3 Ducret (France) 3-1-9 (1,919).

England team: Harry Hughes 2-1-8 (1,030), Norman Webb 1-7-8 (829), Ronnie Lye 1-2-4 (777), Bob Pegden 1-0-0 (514), Bill Carver 0-3-8 (103). England 5th with 86 points.

1956: RIVER SEINE (FRANCE): —————————————————

Jack Carr.

Team: 1 France 39, 2 Belgium 64, 3 Luxembourg 71.

Individual: 1 Cerfontaine (Belgium) 65 fish (1,541 points), 2 Dubuc (France) 66 fish (1,469), 3 Tesse (France) 55 fish (1,410).

England team: Gerry Woodcock, Joe Thorpe, Joe Cooper, Les Cannon, Jack Carr, Sam Buxton. England finished last of seven.

WORLD CHAMPIONSHIP

1957: SMEDEREVO (YUGOSLAVIA): —————————————

Team: 1 Italy 23, 2 Luxembourg 52, 3 France 54.

Individual: 1 Mandelli (Italy) 439 fish (8,780 points), 2 De Angeli (Italy) 382 fish (7,860), 3 Fugazza (Italy) 371 (7,655).

England did not fish.

1958: HUY (BELGIUM): ——————————————————

Norman Webb.

Team: 1 Belgium 29, 2 France 32, 3 Luxembourg 86.

Individual: 1 Garroit (Belgium) 230 fish (3,225 points), 2 Cerfontaine (Belgium) 242 (3,170), 3 Negrignat (France) 225 (3,065).

England team: Harold Harrison (614 points), Norman Webb (565), Tom Burdett (425), Roy Lusby (405), Harold Storey (311). England 6th (score not known).

1959: NEUCHATEL (SWITZERLAND):

Roy Lusby.

Team: 1 France 71, 2 Italy 103, 3 Switzerland 104.

Individual: 1 Tesse (France) 196 fish (6,385 points), 2 De Angeli (Italy) 149 (6,340), 3 Knapen (Holland) 257 (6,105).

England team: Roy Lusby (3,290 points), Bill Hughes (640), Billy Lane (3,095), Harry Wills (4,355), Harold Harrison (1,675). England 8th with 172 points.

1960: GDANSK (POLAND):

Jim Sharp.

Team: 1 Belgium 36, 2 France 61, 3 E. Germany 87.

Individual: 1 Tesse (France) 2,000 pts, 2 Cerfontaine (Belgium) 1,905, Swennen (Belgium) 1,855 (Note: The numbers of fish caught in this match are not known).

England team: Jim Sharp (19 points), Chris Seal (27), L. Lascelles (30), Stan Jenkins (39), Bill Deacon (45). England 7th with 160 points.

1961: MERSEBURG (EAST GERMANY):

Frank Butler.

Team: 1 E. Germany 44, 2 Belgium 65, 3 England 71.

Individual: 1 Legouge (France) 17 fish (3,120 points), 2 Schmidt (E. Germany) 5 (1,830), 3 Tesse (France) 16 (1,720).

England team: Billy Lane (740 points), Don Rowley (240), Eric Broad (220), Frank Butler (110), Lew Barber (no score).

1962: LAKE GARDA (ITALY):

Bernard Donovan.

Team: 1 Italy 24, 2 France 71, 3 Belgium 95.

Individual: 1 Tedesco (Italy) 447 fish (3,615 points), 2 Fontanet (France) 407 (3,093), 3 Vannelli (Italy) 179 (2,865).

England team: Bernard Donovan (1,364 points), David Owen (1,148), Ken Beswick (997), Ken Thompson (864), George Robinson (822). England 6th (score not known).

1963: WORMELDANGE (LUXEMBOURG):

Champion: *Billy Lane.*

Team: 1 France 57, 2 Italy 77, 3 England 80.

Individual: 1 Lane (England) 74 fish (4,570 points), 2 Tesse (France) 85 (3,230), 3 Vannelli (Italy) 45 (2,865).

England team: Billy Lane (1st), Don Rowley (5th), Albert Garfoot (7th), Billy Widdowson (25th), H. Bolton (42nd).

✳Up to this point the European and World team events were decided by adding together the overall placings of each man in matches not fished in sections. From 1964 onwards they were decided on the aggregate of section points.

1964: PESCAROLI (ITALY):

Jimmy Diamond.

Team: 1 France 6, 2 Italy 9, 3 Austria 20

Individual: 1 Fontanet (France) 42 fish (4,720 points), 2 Depres (France) 43 (4.345), 3 Tesse (France) 58 (3,935).

England team: H. Beckett, Charlie Dickinson, Jimmy Diamond, D. Jelley, E. Wych. England 9th (score not known)

1965: GALATI (ROUMANIA): ————————————

Cliff Burch.

Team: 1 Roumania 22, 2 France 27, 3 Poland 32.

Individuals: 1 Tesse (France) 11 fish (3,227 points), 2 Ceppi (Italy) 15 (2,001), 3 Burch (England) 6 (1,998).

England team: Cliff Burch, Charlie Price, Billy Lane, Ron Russell, Roy Walker (points scores not known)
England 9th with 41 points.

✳*Bernard Donovan appointed manager of the England team. NFA Secretary Tom Draper had been in charge of virtually all the preceding matches.*

1966: RIVER THURNE (ENGLAND): ————————————

Dave Burr.

Team: 1 France 11, 2 Belgium 15, 3 Italy 24.

Individual: 1 Guienheuf (France) 74 fish (5.742 points), 2 Baudot (Belgium) 79 (3,868), 3 Roelandt (Belgium) 40 (3,744).

England team: Terry Gardner (3,693 points), Dave Burr (2,302), Ray Hough (1,821), Colin Clough (114), Neil Mumford (379). England 6th with 29 points.

1967: DUNAJVAROS (YUGOSLAVIA): ————————————

Roy Jarvis.

Team: 1 Belgium 12, 2 France 17, 3 England 25.

Individual: 1 Isenbaert (Belgium) 652 fish (9,880 points), 2 Handt (W. Germany) 23 (9,400), 3 Detry (Belgium) 563 (9.160).

England team: Roy Marlow (2 points), Bill Bartles (4), John Pinder (7), Roy Jarvis (1), Brian Hallewell (11).

1968: FERMOY (IRELAND):

Ernie Wilde.

Team: 1 France 18, 2 W. Germany 24, 3 Roumania 25.

Individual: 1 Grebenstein (W. Germany) 20 fish (3,218 points), 2 Pana (Roumania) 45 (2,393), 3 Sherwood (England) 9 (1,689).

England team: Vince Sherwood (2 points), Ernie Wilde (2), Brian Weatherley (2), Mick Howard (11), Frank Holt (8). England 4th with 25 points.

✳The scoring system in world events to date had been based on 5 points per fish and one point for each gramme of weight. The rule was changed after the 1968 event to give just one point for each fish and one for each gramme of weight.

1969: BAD OLDESLOE (WEST GERMANY):

Champion: *Robin Harris.*

Team: 1 Holland 17, 2 Belgium 19, 3 France 21.

Individual: 1 Harris (England) 64 fish (4,462 points), 2 Leyrer (Austria) 58 (2,633), 3 Vermuelen (Belgium) 38 (2,555).

England team: Robin Harris (1 point), George Golding (9), David Groom (8), Hubert Noar (6), Harry Moss (12). England 5th with 36 points.

1970: BERG (HOLLAND):

Albert Rodway.

Team: 1 Belgium 8, 2 Holland 14, 3 France 16.

Individual: 1 Van den Eynde (Belgium) 74 fish (4,084 points), 2 Michiels (Belgium) 58 (3,330), 3 Pacquet (Belgium) 40 (2,967).

England team: Tony Flowers (9 points), Norman Hayes (5), Peter James (6), Albert Rodway (8), Kevin Ashurst (9). England 8th with 37 points.

✳England manager Bernard Donovan died after five years in charge of the team, and Stan Smith was appointed to replace him.

1971: PESCHIERA (ITALY):

Percy Anderson.

Team: 1 Italy 6, 2 Belgium 21, 3 France 16.

Individual: Bassi (Italy) 53 fish (3,913 points), 2 Alfieri (Italy) 44 (2,744), 3 Zimmer (W. Germany) 182 (2,492).

England team: Dave Docwra (14 points), Frank Howse (12), Ian Roffe (9), Percy Anderson (11), Walter Davison (13). England 12th with 59 points.

✳*All World Championship teams to this date were selected on results in the National Championship, with the top five teams nominating one of their anglers, usually the top weight man. The system changes for 1972 onwards, with the team now picked by the manager.*

1972: VSENORY (CZECHOSLOVAKIA):

Ivan Marks.

Team: 1 France 12, 2 England 24, 3 Italy 25.

Individual: 1 Levels (Holland) 80 fish (9,310 points), 2 Thomms (Luxembourg) 67 (7,599), 3 Jacques Tesse (France) 61 (7,290).

England team: Kevin Ashurst (1 point), Robin Harris (1), Jimmy Randell (8), John Parsons (7), Ivan Marks (7).

1973: CHALONS-SUR-SOANE (FRANCE):

Clive Smith.

Team: 1 Belgium 10, 2 France 16, 3 England 26.

Individual: 1 Michiels (Belgium) 69 fish (3,681 points), 2 Van den Eynde (Belgium) 55 (3,681), 3 Hebert (France) 236 (3,321).

England team: Kevin Ashurst (4 points), Ken Giles (2), Robin Harris (7), Ivan Marks (3), Clive Smith (10).

1974: GHENT (BELGIUM):

Tony Scott.

Team: 1 France 18 (12.296g), 2 Italy 18 (11.604g), 3 Holland 21.

Individual: 1 Richter (W. Germany) 6 fish (5,016 points), 2 Mendez-Gomez (Spain) 75 (4,310), 3 Fougeat (France) 179 (3,794).

England team: Kevin Ashurst (6 points), Ivan Marks (8),Tony Scott (5), Ken Giles (10), Bob Tromans (5). England 6th with 34 points.

✻*The 1974 match was the last to be fished under line limit rules*

1975: BYDGOSZCZ (POLAND):

Champion: Ian Heaps.

Team: 1 France 23, 2 England 26 (15.433kg) 3 Belgium 26 (4.257kg).

Individual: 1 Heaps (England) 14 fish (10,234 points) 2 Jacques Tesse (France) 17 (6,717), 3 De Biagi (San Marino) 6 (4,956).

England team: Kevin Ashurst (1 point), Ian Heaps (1), Ivan Marks (3), Terry Payne (16), Tony Scott (5).

1976: LAKE GEORGI TRAIKOV (BULGARIA):

Ken Giles

Team: 1 Italy 7, 2 Bulgaria 20, 3 Austria 27.

Individual: 1 Bassi (Italy) 384 fish (8,269 points), 2 Marks (England) 190 (7,985), 2 Passinetti (Italy) 383 (7,723).

England team: Kevin Ashurst (4 points), Ian Heaps (9), Ken Giles (11), Ivan Marks (2), Tony Scott (9). England 5th with 35 points.

✻*The 1976 match was the first in which the individual match was fished separately, the anglers qualifying on their section placing in the team match. The individual match followed the team event, and was fished for only 90 minutes because they ran out of time. Normally the matches last three hours.*

1977: MOSELLE (LUXEMBOURG):

Dickie Carr.

Team: 1 Luxembourg 16, 2 Belgium 18, 3 France 19.

Individual: 1 Mainil (Belgium) 31 fish (3,941 points), 2 Poth (Luxembourg) 23 (3,153), 3 Quinet (Belgium) 28 (3,128).

England team: Kevin Ashurst (7 points), Ivan Marks (6), Dickie Carr (6), Ian Heaps (1), Tony Scott (10). England 5th with 30 points.

1978: VIENNA (AUSTRIA):

Mark Downes.

Team: 1 France 14, 2 Italy 19, 3 Czechoslovakia 24.

Individual: 1 Fougeat (France) 11 fish (1,561 points), 2 Trabucco (Italy) 96 (1,496), 3 Birnbaum (Luxembourg) (1,487).

England team: Kevin Ashurst (16 points), Ivan Marks (11), Mark Downes (18), Tom Pickering (18), Ian Heaps (18). England 18th and last with 81 points.

1979: ZARAGOZA (SPAIN):

Denis White.

Team: 1 France 14, 2 Holland 16, 3 Portugal 25.

Individual: 1 Heulard (France) 78 fish (2,155 points), 2 Eikhout (Holland) 82 (2,120), 3 Durozier (France) 4 (1,670).

England team: Kevin Ashurst (3 points), Ivan Marks (9), Ian Heaps (12), Denis White (6), Tony Scott (9). England 7th with 39 points.

✱*The one point per fish scoring system ended here. Section results and individual match are now decided on weight only.*

1980: RIVER NECKAR (WEST GERMANY):

Tom Pickering.

Team: 1 Germany 7, 2 England 23, 3 Belgium 24.

Individual: 1 Kremkus (W. Germany) 16,990kg, 2 Wessel (W. Germany) 10.975kg, 3 Trabucco (Italy) 10.830kg.

England team: Kevin Ashurst (1 point), Ian Heaps (8), Ivan Marks (2), Tom Pickering (8), Tony Scott (4).

1981: AVON AT LUDDINGTON (ENGLAND):

Champion: *Dave Thomas.*

Teams: France 25, England 31, Wales 39.

Individual: 1 Thomas (England) 1190kg, 2 Santos (Portugal) 930g, 3 Lecocq (Belgium) 630g.

England team: Clive Smith (13 points), Tony Scott (11), Dave Thomas (1), Kevin Ashurst (3), John Dean (3).

1982: NEWRY CANAL (NORTHERN IRELAND):

Champion: *Kevin Ashurst.*

Team: 1 Holland 20, 2 France 25, 3 England 26.

Individuals: 1 Ashurst (England) 820g, 2 Thill (USA) 680g, 3 Bartolas (Belgium) 580g.

England team: Kevin Ashurst (1 point), Ivan Marks (7), Alan McAtee (6), Dave Brogden (6), Ian Heaps (6).

1983: RHINE CANAL (HOLLAND): _____

Alan McAtee.

Team: 1 Belgium 9, 2 England 14, 3 Holland 24.

Individual: 1 Kremkus (W. Germany) 6.945kg, 2 Kohn (Luxembourg) 6,250kg, 3 Van Gool (Holland) 4.150kg.

England team: Alan McAtee (1 point), Ian Heaps (1), Kevin Ashurst (2), Dave Roper (4), Dickie Carr (6).

✻*After this match Stan Smith was replaced as England manager by Dick Clegg, who was backed by substantial sponsorship by H. Steade & Sons Ltd., the Sheffield firm of keepnet and umbrella manufacturers.*

1984: RIVER THIELLE (SWITZERLAND): _____

Bob Nudd.

Team: 1 Luxembourg 28 (9.410kg), 2 England 28 (7.535kg), 3 Belgium 40.

Individuals: 1 Smithers (Ireland) 8.500kg, 2 Stephens (Scotland) 2.510, 3 Brouwer (Holland) 2.320kg.

England team: Bob Nudd (2 pts), Kevin Ashurst (5), Ian Heaps (5), Denis White (5), Tom Pickering (11).

1985: RIVER ARNO (ITALY): _____

Champion: Dave Roper.

Team: 1 England 16, 2 Italy 17, 3 Belgium 25

Individuals: 1 Roper (England) 6.405kg, 2 Trabucco (Italy) 5.430kg, 3 Davies (Wales) 4.930kg.

England team: Bob Nudd (10 points), Denis White (1), Tom Pickering (1), Ian Heaps (2), Kevin Ashurst (2).

1986: STRASBOURG (FRANCE):

Clive Branson.

Team: 1 Italy 27, 2 W. Germany 27, 3 Austria 40.

Individuals: 1 Wever (Holland) 3.940kg, 2 Branson (Wales) 2.920kg, 3 Van Neer (Holland) 1.730kg.

England Team: Tom Pickering (5 points), Bob Nudd (8), Ian Heaps (12), Denis White (23), Kevin Ashurst (2). England 7th with 50 points, and beaten for the first time by Wales, 6th with 49.

1987: RIVER MONDEGO (PORTUGAL):

Steve Gardener.

Team: 1 England 9, 2 Italy 18, 3 Austria 33.

Individuals: 1 Branson (Wales) 2.500kg, 2 Ashurst (England) 2.485kg, 3 White (England) 2.220kg.

England team: Steve Gardener (3 points), Kevin Ashurst (1), Ian Heaps (2), Denis White (1), Tom Pickering (2).

✻Another rule change. The team event is now to be decided on aggregate section points in two matches, with the individual champion the angler with the best section scores.

1988: DAMME CANAL (BELGIUM):

Vinnie Smith.

Team: 1 England 50 (19.125kg), 2 Italy 50 (14.335kg), 3 France 58.

Individuals: 1 Fougeat (France) 2 points, 2 Gardener (England) 3 (5.270kg), 3 Colombo (Italy) 3 (4.290kg).

England team: Kevin Ashurst (4 and 9 points), Dave Roper (1 and 3), Steve Gardener (2 and 1), Bob Nudd (1 and 5), Vinnie Smith (16 and 8). England tied with Italy on points both days, and won on aggregate weight.

Other Popular books by

PUBLICATIONS

The Young Angler by Dave King
The most comprehensive beginners' guide still in print
(Foreword by Colin Dyson)

Modern Match Fishing by Dave King
A must for the ambitious matchman
(Foreword by Ken Giles)

The Modern Coarse Angler by Dave King
A wealth of basic advice and instruction